SACRAMENTO PUBLIC LIBRARY
3 3029 03314 6515

D0049387

JUST WAR
AND THE
GULF WAR

JAMES TURNER JOHNSON is university director of international programs, professor of religion, and associate member of the graduate department of political science at Rutgers University. A graduate of Brown, he received his B.D. at Vanderbilt and his Ph.D. at Princeton. Among his many scholarly awards are a Rockefeller Foundation Humanities Fellowship (1976) and a Guggenheim Fellowship (1984). Johnson is the editor and author of numerous books including *Ideology, Reason, and the Limitation of War: Secular and Religious Concepts, 1200–1740* (Princeton, 1975), *Just War Tradition and the Restraint of War: A Moral and Historical Inquiry* (Princeton, 1981), *Can Modern War Be Just?* (Yale, 1984), and *The Quest for Peace: Three Moral Traditions in Western Cultural History* (Princeton, 1987).

GEORGE WEIGEL is president of the Ethics and Public Policy Center. A graduate of St. Mary's Seminary and University in Baltimore and the University of St. Michael's College in Toronto, he was a 1984–85 Fellow of the Woodrow Wilson International Center for Scholars. Weigel is the author of seven books, among them *Freedom and Its Discontents: Catholicism Confronts Modernity* (Ethics and Public Policy Center, 1991), *Tranquillitas Ordinis: The Present Failure and Future Promise of American Catholic Thought on War and Peace* (Oxford, 1987), *Catholicism and the Renewal of American Democracy* (Paulist, 1989), and *American Interests, American Purpose: Moral Reasoning and U.S. Foreign Policy* (Praeger, 1989).

JUST WAR AND THE GULF WAR

James Turner Johnson
George Weigel

ETHICS AND PUBLIC POLICY CENTER

The **ETHICS AND PUBLIC POLICY CENTER,** established in 1976, conducts a program of research, writing, publications, and conferences to encourage debate on domestic and foreign policy issues among religious, educational, academic, business, political, and other leaders. A nonpartisan effort, the Center is supported by contributions (which are tax deductible) from foundations, corporations, and individuals. The authors alone are responsible for the views expressed in Center publications.

Library of Congress Cataloging-in-Publication Data

Johnson, James Turner.
Just war and the Gulf war / James Turner Johnson.
p. cm.
Includes bibliographical references and index.
1. Persian Gulf War, 1991—Religious aspects.
2. Just war doctrine. I. Weigel, George. II. Title.
DS79.72.J64 1991
956.704' 3—dc20 91–27677 CIP

ISBN 0–89633–166–0 (hardcover : alk. paper)

Distributed by arrangement with:

University Press of America, Inc.
4720 Boston Way
Lanham, MD 20706

3 Henrietta Street
London WC2E 8LU England

All Ethics and Public Policy Center books are produced on acid-free paper. The paper used in this publication meets the minimum requirements of American National Standard for Information Sciences—Permanence of Paper for Printed Library Materials, ANSI Z39.48–1984. ♾™

© 1991 by the Ethics and Public Policy Center. All rights reserved.
Printed in the United States of America.

Ethics and Public Policy Center
1015 Fifteenth Street N.W.
Washington, D.C. 20005
(202) 682–1200

Contents

Preface vii

Part One: Was the Gulf War a Just War?

The Just War Tradition and the American Military
James Turner Johnson 3

Part Two: The Churches and the Gulf Crisis

War, Peace, and the Christian Conscience
George Weigel 45

Part Three: Key Documents

1 Message from the Executive Coordinating Committee of the National Council of the Churches of Christ in the U.S.A., September 14, 1990 93

2 Letter from Archbishop Roger Mahony to Secretary of State James Baker, November 7, 1990 99

3 Message and Resolution from the General Board of the National Council of the Churches of Christ in the U.S.A., November 15, 1990 105

4 Letter from Archbishop Daniel Pilarczyk to President George Bush, November 15, 1990 113

5 Testimony of Archbishop John Roach Before the Senate Foreign Relations Committee, December 6, 1990 117

6 Statement from Eighteen Church Leaders to the American People, December 21, 1990 131

7 Message from Thirty-two Church Leaders to President George Bush, January 15, 1991 137

8 Address by President George Bush to the National Religious Broadcasters, January 28, 1991 141

9 Statement to the Press by Jim Wallis, February 1, 1991 147

10 A Call to the Churches, February 12, 1991 153

Notes 159

Index of Names 165

Preface

A mere ten months ago, after the Revolution of 1989 and the demise of the Cold War, one would have been making a risky wager indeed to have suggested that the American body politic would soon be enmeshed in a lengthy and passionate public moral debate about the just war tradition and its utility in the modern world.

Yet that is precisely what happened when the Gulf War began with Saddam Hussein's invasion of Kuwait on August 2, 1990. This small book is a reflection on the just war debate over the Gulf crisis and an attempt to clarify the relevant issues for the future of the argument over the morally appropriate use of military force in the pursuit of peace, justice, freedom, security, and order. For we can be certain that the argument will continue. History has not ended—not by a long shot.

A brief description of the book's contents may be helpful. James Turner Johnson's essay explores the recent history of the evolving just war tradition, discusses the presence of the tradition in international law and American military doctrine, and analyzes the conduct of the Gulf War according to the classic moral criteria of the tradition. George Weigel's essay examines the American religious community's contributions—for good and for ill—to the public moral debate over U.S. policy in the Gulf and suggests how the concept of peace embedded in the just war tradition (understood as a theory of statecraft) might be applied to the tangled affairs of the Middle East.

Part Three of the book is devoted to documentation. The Gulf War debate generated a considerable amount of formal commentary from the National Council of Churches, the United States Catholic Conference, and other religious agencies. The debate also engaged the White House. We thought it useful to preserve these documents for the sake of the historical record and, in some instances, as a cautionary tale.

We believe that the just war tradition will remain an indispensable resource for morally concerned citizens trying to think through America's role in a world that is, at one and the same time, increasingly united and divided. Our hope is that this book may contribute to a deepening of the public conversation about war and peace, a conversation that inevitably involves profound issues of good and evil, of right and wrong, for individual citizens as well as for the nation.

JAMES TURNER JOHNSON
GEORGE WEIGEL

June 1991

Part One

Was the Gulf War a Just War?

The Just War Tradition and the American Military

James Turner Johnson

MUCH MORAL debate in American society takes place in arguments over politics, economics, social policy, the application of technology, and other such subjects. This is as it should be, since moral concerns, properly understood, relate to all arenas of human activity. Of particular relevance to this book is the fact that, despite the efforts of political realists to dissociate the practice of statecraft from ethics, American political debate over the use of military force is full of arguments and appeals rooted in moral concerns. Indeed, far from being irrelevant to the political process, such concerns have historically played a major role in American political life. Americans want their nation's actions to be moral; it is part of the legacy of that tradition by which this country is "a city set on a hill," a model for other nations to follow.

Exactly how the moral element should express itself in political policies, decisions, and actions is the stuff of abundant discussion and the motivation for much activity in the public sphere. For the moral element is not a seamless web; it is expressed through a variety of types of claims drawn from diverse sources and supported by a multitude of reference points. It is no less powerful for that; rather, this variety simply testifies to the freedom and independence Americans enjoy within their social and political structures. To acknowledge such diversity is not to say that we cannot make distinctions among the merits of various moral claims and arguments. Indeed, making such distinctions, and thereby adding to the moral clarity of the issues at stake, is itself part of the contribution that ethical analysis has to make to the exercise of statecraft.

This essay examines one particular element in the moral debate over American use of military force against Iraq in the Gulf War: the justifiability of that action in terms of the just war tradition of Western culture. This tradition has deep roots in both the ancient Hebraic and the classical Greek and Roman foundations of the West. It has developed over history in both religious and non-religious strands and takes contemporary form in religious doctrine, in international law on war, in codes of military conduct, and in underlying values regarding human rights and the rights of nations.[1]

The Language of Morality

Just war claims were much in evidence in the debate over American involvement in the 1990–91 Gulf War. "This is a just war," President Bush told the convention of the National Religious Broadcasters.[2] "I fear that . . . the undertaking of offensive military action [by the United States against Iraq] could well violate [just war] criteria," declared Archbishop Daniel Pilarczyk, president of the National Conference of Catholic Bishops.[3] His colleague, Archbishop John Roach, spelled out before the Senate Foreign Relations Committee the criteria for a just war as understood in Catholic teaching.[4] The *Christian Century* published a debate on "Just War Tradition and the War in the Gulf,"[5] and the American Society of Christian Ethics adopted a resolution on the war that explicitly invoked Christian just war reasoning. The religion editor of the *New York Times* wrote several columns on this subject, which was also a focus for treatment in other newspapers, television and radio commentary, and the national newsmagazines.

These were some of the direct references to the idea of just war. But clearly articulated concepts of what makes the use of military force justified or unjustified were also evident in the debates that took place within the United Nations Security Council and the U.S. Congress. Both the explicit and the implicit reliance on the language of justice and morality reveal the vigor of a moral tradition whose roots go deep into Western cultural history, but whose modern development has extended to the moral traditions of other cultures as well. Every culture has a moral tradition that addresses the justification and limitation of war. Though the specific terms and structures of what has come to be called just war tradition are those that have taken shape in the West, their ideas represent a far broader concept of the moral uses and limits of military force.

For our present purposes, we will remain within the framework of just war ideas as they have taken shape in Western cultural history, for this is the context within which the American debate has developed. This tradition provides us with categories for moral reflection about war, peace, and statecraft; it also gives us tools to evaluate the contents of those categories: notions of right and wrong, justice and injustice in international affairs; of the justified use of force within the purposes of statecraft, including as an ultimate goal the end of peace; and of limits on justified use of force.

There is a classic, systematic form of just war theory, and I will return to it below when I outline my own moral judgments on the use of military force against Iraq. But since just war ideas are also employed in looser, less systematic ways in American moral and political discourse, I will turn to these first.

Just War and Pacifism

Just war claims in the American tradition are often set over against arguments drawn from some form of pacifism; frequently the two issues are mixed, with just war reasoning used to support a pacifist rejection of the use of force as an instrument of national policy. Some theorists[6] impute to just war theory a presumption against violence, a view that would align it with certain kinds of contemporary pacifism. Yet historically just war tradition rests on a different presumption, a fundamental rejection of injustice. The use of violent force may be right or wrong depending on whether it serves justice or injustice: hence the idea of "just" or "justified" war. Nor do all forms of pacifism stem from a rejection of violence; the sectarian pacifism of the earliest Christians, medieval monasticism, and the radical pacifist groups of the Reformation era arose out of an animus against secular society as a whole, not just its violent aspects.[7] Just war theory and pacifism are thus distinct moral traditions, and pacifist arguments must be assessed on their own terms, not confused with just war reasoning.[8]

"The use of power, and possibly the use of force, is of the *esse* of politics," wrote Paul Ramsey, whose works on Christian just war theory in the 1960s were a major contribution to contemporary moral reflection on military issues in American politics. Ramsey noted:

> At the same time the use of power, and possibly the use of force, is inseparable from the *bene esse* of politics, . . . inseparable from politics' *proper* act of being politics, inseparable from the well-being of politics, inseparable from the human pursuit of the national or the international common good by political means. You never have *good* politics without the use of power, possibly armed force.[9]

In a later essay, Ramsey turned the matter around, stressing the inseparability of ethics from politics:

> Ethics are not logically, externally related to politics. These two distinguishable elements are together in the first place, internally related. Our quest should be for the clarification of political ethics in its *specific* nature, for the ethical ingredient inherent in foreign policy formulation, for the wisdom peculiar to taking counsel amid a world of encountering powers, for—as a subset—the laws of war and of deterrence so long as these are human activities properly related and subordinated to the purposes of political communities in the international system.[10]

It is just this connection between the possibility of good politics and the possibility of the use of force that just war tradition presumes in theory and seeks to establish in fact; pacifism rejects out of hand the possibility of such a connection. The inherent nature of this connection is apparent in the various strains within the just war tradition—religious elements, including both theology and canonical rules of conduct; secular elements, including theoretical, customary, and positive international law, political philosophy, military codes of conduct, and the historical practice of limitation in war; and other lines of development of lesser scope and importance.[11]

A Varied and Complex Tradition

The historical development of these various carriers of just war tradition resembles the changing waterways of a river delta: now the major streams flow apart, now they mingle their waters, now they part again and recombine with other streams. In this way each of the distinguishable elements within the larger tradition is related to all the others and to the whole, while manifesting its own particular perspective on justice in the use of military force. The just war tradition, understood as encompassing all these streams of development, constitutes the major Western cultural effort to define and explore the ethical justifications and limitations of the use of military force as a proper tool of political activity. As James Childress argues, it establishes the categories of moral reason when considering the use of force and lays down *prima facie* duties to be observed in that use.[12] It is thus not surprising that Americans debating the morality of American involvement in the Gulf War should have had recourse to this tradition in seeking to understand their country's obligations and rights, and in seeking to justify their conclusions about the proper course of action for the United States to follow.

In American public life, then, there is both a history of the application of moral concerns to political questions and a deep moral tradition addressing the notion of just use of force in the service of statecraft. More specifically, during the Gulf crisis the terms and conditions of just war thinking were set by developments that took place within three major carriers of just war tradition in recent history. Each of these needs to be sketched out in turn: developments in Christian just war doctrine in debate over nuclear arms and deterrence and over U.S. involvement in the Vietnam War; developments in international law regarding efforts to outlaw aggression, to prevent crimes against humanity, and to strengthen the law of war; and developments in American military doctrine and capabilities as they may be applied to limiting and making more discriminate the destructiveness of war.

Christian Just War Thinking

Paul Ramsey's 1961 *War and the Christian Conscience*[13] provides a major benchmark for understanding the recent development of Christian just war thought. In this work, which sought to counter what Ramsey perceived as a growing Christian contextualism as well as a widespread argument that Christianity is inherently pacifist, Ramsey argued that Christian just war theory is based on the moral duty of love of neighbor. The obligation to protect the neighbor who is being unjustly attacked provides justification for Christians to resort to force; at the same time, love also imposes limits on such force, requiring that no more be done to the unjust assailant than is necessary to prevent the evil he would do, and that no justified use of force ever can itself directly and intentionally target the innocent. Christian just war theory, argued Ramsey, is thus "twin-born," with limitation accompanying justification of resort to force. At the same time, the specifically Christian character of the just war idea as developed by Ramsey led to a focus on issues the classic just war tradition had called the *ius in bello*, those having to do with right conduct in the *use* of force, and a general neglect of the other aspect of the classic tradition, the *ius ad bellum*, regarding the justification of *resort* to force.

The Challenge of Nuclear Weapons

Focusing especially on the *ius in bello* principle of discrimination—the requirement that noncombatants not be directly and intentionally attacked—Ramsey in the latter part of *War and the Christian Conscience* developed a powerful argument against nuclear deterrence by counter-population (later called "counter-value") targeting. At the same time, he did not oppose nuclear weapons in principle, stating that counter-force uses of such weapons, observing the principle of discrimination, were not morally objectionable. In essays later written and collected in *The Just War*[14] he extended this argument, taking into account developments in both nuclear weapons and strategic thought and, as the American involvement in the Vietnam War deepened, moral issues in the conduct of that war.

These two works by Ramsey were genuinely seminal. At the time these books were being written, the heirs of Reinhold Niebuhr's Christian realism were fighting over its implications for the nuclear age, and except for these there were no other

Christian ethical theorists besides Ramsey addressing in specifically Christian terms the justification and limitation of the use of military force in the service of statecraft. Ramsey's emphasis on an absolutely binding ethical requirement of love as the basis for Christian thinking about war effectively countered his contextualist adversaries, making it necessary for them to consider moral issues related to the use of force in other than merely prudential terms. Simultaneously, his insistence that in certain circumstances Christian love imposes a positive requirement of resort to force also provided a strong rebuttal to the Christian pacifist position that love mandates that one never participate in violence. Thus Ramsey gave Christian just war thinking a new and forceful dimension that has decisively shaped, for good and for ill, subsequent debate by both just war theorists and pacifists.

An Overemphasis on Discrimination

An unfortunate side of Ramsey's reconstruction of just war thought was his avoidance of *ius ad bellum* issues. This was not accidental; he regarded them as matters of practical political judgment and thus outside the sphere of competence of Christian moral theorists like himself.[15] The problem with this line of thinking is that, when coupled with Ramsey's stress on the absoluteness of the principle of discrimination, it had the effect of introducing a new *ius ad bellum* based on the test of discrimination alone, rather than basing justification for force on the need to serve an innocent neighbor under unjust attack. Ramsey never addressed the dilemma posed by the possibility that his "twin-born" bases of Christian just war theory might conflict: how does the Christian respond to the love-based obligation to protect the neighbor when the only way of doing so would require action that violates the requirement of discrimination?[16]

Nuclear pacifists such as the British theorist Walter Stein

and, more recently, John Finnis and others resolved this dilemma in favor of the principle of discrimination.[17] Arguing that nuclear warfare could never satisfy this absolute moral requirement, they reasoned backwards that war in the nuclear age is not justified: the absence of compliance with the *ius in bello* thus became a denial that there could ever be a *ius ad bellum*, a justification for resort to force in the service of the ends of statecraft. Others, especially during the Vietnam era, extended this reasoning still further to the position of "modern-war" pacifism, arguing that the nature of warfare in the contemporary age is to be inherently indiscriminate and disproportionately destructive in its effects. This argument is sometimes extended still further to moral opposition to "militarism," a somewhat elastic term for what is perceived as too great a presence of the military in American and other societies.[18]

Contributions of the Bishops

In 1983 the American Catholic bishops added another benchmark document to the development of recent Christian just war thought: their pastoral letter, *The Challenge of Peace*. The principal drafter of this document, Fr. J. Bryan Hehir, characterized his efforts as an attempt to stand between the positions of Ramsey and Stein; the result was the rejection of any use of nuclear weapons (nuclear pacifism), strong reservations about any non-nuclear resort to force in the service of national policy (modern-war pacifism), but acceptance of nuclear weapons for the purpose of deterrence until some better way could be found to deter war.[19] Despite the inherent tensions—according to some critics, contradictions—in this position,[20] it has had great influence as a statement of contemporary Christian just war thought.

Where *The Challenge of Peace* most clearly went beyond Ramsey's version of Christian just war thinking was in its effort to relate its argument to the historical Christian just war tradition and in its explicit statement of just war criteria in a form that drew on the classical *ius ad bellum* and not only the *ius in bello*.[21] While the resulting list of criteria does not precisely match the listing that can be derived from earlier sources,[22] it would have represented an important advance in the contemporary Christian use of just war tradition were it not for its underlying pacifist assumption. In addition to rejecting any war involving nuclear weapons and holding strong reservations against even non-nuclear war today, *The Challenge of Peace* erroneously established Christian just war teaching on a presumption against violence.[23] The general effect is to make it so difficult to conceive of a possible use of force justified in Christian terms that the bishops verge on a pacifist rejection of all contemporary war, whatever the reason.

A great deal of the Christian argumentation against American use of military force against Iraq in the Gulf crisis is at least consistent with modern-war pacifism. What the Catholic bishops' version of Christian just war thought does is to skew the moral tradition in favor of making *ius in bello* considerations—or, more accurately, the *expectation* that *ius in bello* considerations will be violated—do the work for which classic just war tradition developed the *ius ad bellum*. This is a grave error, as I will attempt to show.

Developments in International Law

In the medieval period, the developing just war tradition functioned as the "international law" of European societies. Modern international law emerged out of the broader tradition in the sixteenth and seventeenth centuries, paralleling the growth of the modern state system. Throughout the modern period international law has served as one of the major carriers of just war tradition and has developed elements of that tradition in distinctive and significant ways.[24]

Beginning with the Geneva Convention of 1864, gaining momentum with the Brussels Declaration of 1874, and continuing through the two Hague Conferences of 1899 and 1907 and a succession of Geneva Conventions through the Protocols of 1977, positive international law has laid down concrete guidelines and regulations specifying the requirements of the *ius in bello* and imposing sanctions for failure to observe them. "Geneva law" in general defines the requirements of noncombatant immunity or the principle of discrimination in terms of specific forms of treatment to be given to particular classes of persons during a war. "Hague law" in turn treats the means and methods of warfare, addressing in general the requirements of the principle of proportionality.

To the specific rules and categories established here, the Nuremberg Trials at the end of World War II added a more extensive category, that of "crimes against humanity," with both *ius in bello* and *ius ad bellum* implications. Commenting on the state of international law on war twenty-five years after Nuremberg, Tom J. Farer summarized the contents of that law as expressing three fundamental principles: discrimination or noncombatant immunity, proportionality, and "no Carthaginian peace."[25] The first two of these principles, of course, coincide with the broader tradition and parallel Ramsey's *ius in bello* discussed above. In the broader tradition the concept of "no Carthaginian peace"—that is, no destruction during war that would leave the battle area sterile and uninhabitable after the war is over—is generally collapsed into the protection due noncombatants, for after a war is done all are noncombatants.[26] Nonetheless, Farer's way of encapsulating the requirements laid down in the international law version of *ius in bello* has the advantage of emphasizing that what is justifiable in a war must be assessed in terms of its long-term consequences, not just its immediate effects.

Ius in Bello v. Ius ad Bellum

The implications of the international law *ius in bello* figured importantly in the Gulf crisis in three major ways: (1) judging the actions of the Iraqi occupying forces in Kuwait, (2) determining the parameters within which the coalition forces should operate in employing force against Iraq, and (3) assessing the actions of both sides during the coalition offensive of January 1991, including the intentional destruction undertaken by the retreating Iraqi forces.

In the matter of the *ius ad bellum*, international law generally is somewhat narrower than the just war tradition as a whole. Nonetheless, this relatively narrow focus has the advantage of bringing greater clarity and specificity to the matters involved. The early theorists of international law, beginning with Grotius in the seventeenth century, wrote in the aftermath of a century of terribly destructive and indiscriminate wars of religion, and they sought to block the recurrence of such warfare (what we would call "ideological war") by deemphasizing those portions of the inherited *ius ad bellum* of just war tradition that were capable of being used for ideological purposes.[27]

Their tactic had three components: reducing the allowable means of going to war to those of concrete national interest; emphasizing a formal declaration of war and a public account of the reasons to allow the international community to assess the decision; and stressing the requirement (inherited from the broader just war tradition) that only national sovereigns possess the authority to make war. The revised international law theory of *ius ad bellum* succeeded in dampening resort to ideological warfare, but it opened the way for the development of the idea that any state enjoyed *compétence de guerre* and could decide at any time whether to go to war for its own national interests, as it alone defined them. The result was the period of limited but frequent "sovereigns' wars" in the eighteenth century. Ideological warfare, with its tendency toward totalistic means, again raised its head in the period of the French Revolution and the Napoleonic Wars, and the "sovereigns' war" idea resurfaced at the end of the nineteenth century, culminating in the Great War—World War I.

Efforts of International Organizations

Following the First World War the League of Nations sought to introduce new restrictions into the international law *ius ad bellum* by establishing international arbitration as an intermediary step to be taken before a conflict escalated into armed hostilities. In 1928 a further step was taken in the Pact of Paris, which sought to eliminate recourse to war as a means of settling international disputes. What was condemned was in fact *first* resort to armed force; defensive *second* resort was, the Pact's chief proponents made clear, in no way restricted.

These inter-war efforts did not prevent World War II, which combined the worst features of the patterns of ideological warfare and "sovereigns' war." The subsequent war-crimes trials at Nuremberg and Tokyo and the establishment of a new international order in the form of the United Nations sought to restrict still further the existing *ius ad bellum* in international law. This was to be accomplished by strengthening the measures taken in the Covenant of the League of Nations (which set up structures for international arbitration and legal judgment to settle disputes without war) and in enacting the Pact of Paris (which restricted first, i.e., aggressive, resort to military force while permitting second, i.e., defensive, use of such force). The Nuremberg Trials reinforced this effort by extending the concept of "crime against humanity" to initiating aggressive war. Subsequent United Nations debate and international experience of warfare after 1945 clarified the concepts of aggression and defense.

Thus in August 1990, the *ius ad bellum* of international law was authoritatively defined by Articles 2 and 51 of the United Nations Charter: Article 2 prohibited member nations "from the threat or use of force against the territorial integrity or political independence of any state" and empowered the Security Council to preserve peace; Article 51 granted to all nations, acting individually or collectively, the right to resist with force an "armed attack" until the Security Council "takes the necessary measures to restore international peace and security."

Military Doctrine and Capabilities

Historical experience is an important element in the formation of moral consciousness. Two aspects of the experience of military life have been especially important for the development of just war tradition: the growth of a concept of moral identity on the part of people in military life, a concept that translates into standards of how to act in war; and the encounter with war itself, which affects decisions about strategy, tactics, appropriate weapons, and appropriate uses of those weapons. In both these respects the development of just war tradition has been influenced by military factors and, in turn, the broader tradition has shaped the moral identity of military personnel and their way of understanding the moral meaning of war.

In the Middle Ages, for example, the growth of the chivalric code played an important role in forming a consensus on noncombatant immunity, and this knightly code was, in turn, refined and extended by the influence of Christian moral theology and canon law. As for the encounter with war itself, the development of limited war as a norm in the eighteenth century was a direct reflection of the emphasis on *ius in bello* concerns by the moralists and international publicists of the period; in turn, the practice of limited war established empirical standards by which to judge the appropriateness of given means of war and targets in war.[28]

In the contemporary American military context, the concept of moral identity is closely associated with the various service manuals on the law of war and the rules of engagement laid down for a particular situation of the use of military force. The key role played by air power in the war against Iraq and the relevant U.S. Air Force manual, AFP 110–31 (which is the most recently revised service manual on the law of war), are useful reference points for assessing the military component of the just war debate over American use of force in the recent Gulf crisis. The growing reliance on "smart" weapons and battle by maneuver rather than by mutual attrition also provided a reference point for judging whether the Gulf War would proceed within the framework of the criteria of discrimination and proportionality. I will treat these in turn.

Lessons of the Military Manuals

The U.S. military service manuals on the law of war do not treat the question of resort to war; that is a matter for civilian authority to decide. They focus instead on the *ius in bello*, the limits within which military force may be applied. For AFP 110–31, these limits are defined by the principles of humanity and military necessity.

> Military necessity is the principle which justifies measures of regulated force not forbidden by international law, which are indispensable for securing the prompt submission of the enemy, with the least possible expenditures of economic resources. This concept has four basic elements: (i) that the force used is capable of being and is in fact regulated by the user; (ii) that the use of force is necessary to achieve as quickly as possible the . . . submission of the adversary; (iii) that the force used is no greater . . . than needed to achieve his prompt submission (economy of force); and (iv) that

the force used is not otherwise prohibited. . . . Complementing the principle of necessity . . . is the principle of humanity, which forbids the infliction of suffering, injury, or destruction not actually necessary for the accomplishment of legitimate military purposes [the principle of proportionality of means]. . . . The principle of humanity also confirms the basic immunity of civilian populations and civilians from being objects of attack during armed conflict [the principle of discrimination]. This immunity does not preclude unavoidable incidental civilian casualties which may occur during the course of attacks against military objectives, and which are not excessive in relation to the concrete and direct military advantage anticipated.[29]

Thus the fundamental principles of the *ius in bello* of the just war tradition are stated explicitly in the Air Force's manual as defining the parameters for legitimate acts of war. The role of this manual is not simply to lay out rules for conduct, however; this and the other service manuals on the same topic also provide a reference point for the definition of a professional military ethic and for a moral identity appropriate for a member of the services. As the prospect of armed conflict with Iraq neared, the American military services considered their own role in the conflict in terms such as those in the passage quoted above. Their military planning proceeded in this context. The tradition of just war is evident in authoritative policy statements bearing on who the members of the services are to be and how they are to act in case of armed conflict. However popular the Rambo image may be on the movie screen, it is not the image by which the services seek to define themselves and their mission in peace and war.

Encounters and Associations With War

It is a well-worn cliché that armies and their leaders always prepare to fight the last war, never the next one. In the case of American military preparedness in the Gulf crisis, this was emphatically untrue, though it was taken for granted by a considerable segment of American civilian society. The "last war" for some critics was Vietnam, and the corresponding expectation was a lingering, indecisive presence of American forces in the Gulf region as other coalition members drifted away or became alienated. The "last war" for others was World War II, a conflict that spread to engulf nation after nation and whose prosecution led to strategies, tactics, and eventually weapons of mass destruction.

Influencing both of these "last war" conceptions of what to expect in the Gulf was a new myth, expressed by such authors as Paul Fussell and Michael Herr,[30] that modern war is *by its nature* grossly and disproportionately destructive, beyond rational control, and inherently at odds with any reasonable political purpose. Preoccupied with the American experience in Vietnam and with the debate over nuclear deterrence, many critics of the U.S. military have used these images to undergird a general opposition to the use of military force by this country—that is, a moral position of modern-war pacifism coupled at times with a more generalized aversion to things military.

Others involved in the moral debates over military policy in the last thirty years have argued, rather, that wars *can* be waged while avoiding means and methods that are grossly and disproportionately destructive, beyond rational control, and at odds with reasonable political purpose. Those—including myself—who share this view have argued that the Fussell-Herr myth of modern war is simply the wrong way to think about moral responsibility in warfare, and that this responsibility implies developing weapons, strategies, and tactics for war-fighting that allow for use of military force according to the limits given in just war tradition.

Fighting the War at Hand

The influence of this view, combined with two new historical developments, enabled the American military to enter the

Gulf crisis prepared to fight the war at hand—not the "last war," however conceived. The two new elements were the all-volunteer army, which necessitated planning that emphasized training and tactics designed to minimize risk to the scarce and costly human resources available under arms; and new technologies that made possible highly mobile, precise weaponry ideally suited to the concepts developed in the historical experience of limited war: limitation by ends, targets, and means.

When Iraq invaded Kuwait in August 1990, American military doctrine and capabilities were in a state of readiness that was clearly not realized by the majority of Americans, many of whom still thought in terms of the images of World War II, the nuclear age, and the experience of Vietnam. They failed to recognize the degree to which their forces were prepared to wage war within the framework of the just war *ius in bello*—relying on moral identity, exemplified by the manuals of the laws of war and the rules of engagement adopted for the crisis, and on military capabilities, exemplified by the incorporation of "smart weapons," enemy intelligence-suppression means and tactics, and a highly mobile force that used its agility to protect the scarce human resources of the American military.

Justifiable Resort to Force

Examining the Gulf War in just war terms requires standing back from the narrowly political, economic, and ideological arguments that were advanced between August 2 and January 16 and concentrating instead on the implications of the criteria for judgment contained in this moral tradition. The conclusions reached by applying these criteria for judgment include concern for the political, the economic, and the ideological, and bear implications for them; yet just war analysis does not reduce to them, singly or together.

The just war tradition is concerned primarily with the questions of when force is justified in the context of statecraft, and what restraints should be observed in this justifiable use of force. Paul Ramsey has called these the questions of *permission* and *limitation*, respectively. Classically, the moral criteria developed for guidance on the resort to force are known collectively by the Latin term *ius ad bellum*, while the moral criteria on restraint in war form the *ius in bello*.

The just war tradition has arrived at seven criteria that must be satisfied to justify resort to military force. These include just cause, right authority for the use of such force, right intention, the goal of restoring peace, overall proportionality of good over evil, a reasonable hope of success, and a situation of last resort. I will define each criterion more fully, and then examine each in the context of the decision to use force against Iraq.

The Notion of Just Cause

Just cause classically included one or more of three conditions: defense against an attack, recovery of something wrongly taken, or punishment of evil. These terms derive from Roman law and practice and were incorporated into the developing Christian moral theory of justified war by Saint Augustine in the early fifth century.[31] In the Middle Ages the idea of punishment of evil was stressed by thinkers like Thomas Aquinas, who cited as their warrant Romans 13:4: "For [the prince] does not bear the sword in vain; he is the servant of God to execute his wrath on the evildoer."[32]

In order to avoid defining evil in ideological terms, recent just war theorists have tended to focus on one particular evil, the aggressive use of force by a people or nation against another. There has been a corresponding tendency to emphasize defense against ongoing or imminent attack as the primary or only just cause for resort to force. This is clearly the case in contemporary international law, as provided in Articles 2 and 51 of the United Nations Charter. Yet it should not be thought that the earlier notions—of recovery of something wrongly taken, and punishment of evil—have evaporated from the tradition; rather, they have been subsumed within a gradually broadened concept of defense that allows retaliation for an attack launched and completed (punishment of evil) and defines wrongful occupation of territory as a state of "continuing" armed attack.

When Iraq invaded Kuwait on August 2, 1990, and declared that the territory that was "formerly Kuwait" was "irrevocably" part of Iraq, a just cause for use of force against Iraq came into being. This was a flagrant case of aggression, one that violated the most fundamental norms of international order, and it was quickly recognized as such by the United States, by the United Nations Security Council, and also by the overwhelming majority of nations of the world. Not only did Iraq's action blatantly violate the letter of Article 2 of the U. N. Charter (prohibiting "use of force against the territorial integrity [and] political independence" of another country), but, more profoundly, it showed utter disregard for the very norm on which the state system, and through it the United Nations itself, stands: a *de facto* acceptance of every state's right to exist.

The presence of just cause alone is not sufficient to justify resort to force; yet this was as clear and unambiguous a case as one could hope to find in the real world, and the brazenness of Iraq's action remained on public display even as the international community tried to expel the Iraqis through a variety of non-military means.

Critics of the use of force against Iraq cited as (at least partial) justification of Iraq's action various forms of "aggression" employed by Kuwait against Iraq: notably, keeping oil prices lower than was advantageous to Iraq and allegedly pumping oil from Iraqi territory by horizontal drilling. Even if these charges were true, such actions clearly fell far short of the magnitude necessary to justify military retaliation. Rather, conflicts of this sort are to be dealt with by negotiation and arbitration; that is what the very idea of a "world order" conveys.

Action by Right Authority

The second criterion for justified use of force is that such action be undertaken by a *right authority*. In historical terms, this meant a genuinely sovereign prince, that is, one with no political superior. In its early development, the principal function of this criterion was to limit the use of force to those who would rightly employ it, declaring illegitimate any use of force by subordinate nobles, private soldiers, criminals, and even the church. In the modern period the criterion of right authority still seeks to minimize the frequency of resort to force, by limiting it to the political leadership of a sovereign state duly authorized by the legitimate political processes of that state. (The concept of such authority has been extended also to the U.N. Security Council under the conditions specified in the Charter.)

In the case of the Gulf War, right authority for use of force by the coalition of nations cooperating to undo Iraq's aggression was manifest at both the international and national levels. Internationally, such authority was provided by Resolution 678 of the United Nations Security Council. Within the United States, right authority derived first from the president's powers as defined by the Constitution and the War Powers Act, then by the congressional resolutions adopted on January 12 and 13 authorizing use of U.S. military force against Iraq.

Underlying such legal authority is a moral basis for the notion that right authority may use force to serve justice in the international arena. That moral claim is expressed in the same biblical passage, Romans 13:4, that medieval theorists cited to define the idea of justified cause. This passage also embodies an understanding that persons in positions of political authority have a responsibility to uphold the moral order as such, for without it human community would not be possible. This responsibility is not specifically religious or Western—though it is clearly present both in biblical religion and in the political traditions on which Western societies are founded—but is rather a universal concept, the basis of the idea of "world order" that undergirds international law and the United Nations system. Even if it were exclusively religious or Western, this concept of the responsibilities stemming from legitimate political authority would still impose a moral obligation on the political leadership of the American people and on the American people themselves.

Aspects of Right Intention

Right intention, the third notion bearing on the just war decision to resort to force, was classically defined in two ways: positively, by considering whether the other just war criteria were present; and negatively, by distinguishing itself from *wrong* intentions such as those enumerated by Augustine: "the love of violence, revengeful cruelty, fierce and implacable enmity, wild resistance and the lust for power, and such like."[33] In the Middle Ages the requirement of right intention was taken especially seriously as a duty for individuals in combat; soldiers were obligated to do penance after battle in case they had fought with forbidden motivations in their hearts. In the modern period the concept of right intention has become a matter of the conduct of states, not the moral attitudes of individuals. It centers, positively, on such goals as protection or restoration of national, civil, and human rights and other values, reestablishment of order and stability, and the promotion of peace. Negatively, right intention today involves avoiding taking another state's territory, violating the rights of individuals or nations, and deliberately depriving a nation of peace and stability.

All these conditions existed when the United States and allied forces decided to take military action against Iraq. While critics sought to portray U.S. involvement in terms of "blood for oil" or as an effort to secure American hegemony in the Gulf region, such charges ignore the naked act of military aggression (and not the first such act on the part of Iraq) that brought the conflict into being. These critics also assumed bad faith on the part of U.S. and coalition leaders who insisted that their goals were simply to restore Kuwait as a nation and to require Iraq to make amends for damage it caused. Clearly, the subsequent military operation by coalition forces kept to these goals. Indeed, so off-base were the critics in depicting larger motives that, looking back on the internal bloodbath and repression that has swept over Iraq after the international cease-fire, one may wonder whether a broader "right intention" might not, in fact, have been justified: deposition of the dictator Saddam Hussein and creation of the conditions for participatory government in Iraq as a way of serving the human and political rights of the Iraqi people.

The Goal of Peace

The existence of a right intention on the part of the coalition in this case also substantially satisfied the requirement that the use of force *aim at achieving peace*. This criterion was understood classically in terms of three values: order, justice, and peace. The first aim of good politics, according to this view, is an order that reflects the natural law, that is, one that establishes things the way they *ought* to be. This would lead naturally to the existence of justice: a good order is inherently a just one, and maintaining justice protects the right ordering of affairs and relationships within the political community. The establishment of order and justice together produces the third political goal: peace. Peace would flow not only from the right ordering of politics within a society, but from the creation or restoration of a just political order in the relationships within, between, and among nations.

In the case of the Gulf War, the goal of peace was closely tied to the concept of right intention: rolling back Iraqi aggression and restoring Kuwaiti territory and sovereignty (right order and justice), deterring such aggression in the future, restoring the shattered peace of the region, and attempting to set in place safeguards to protect that peace in the future. I will return to this subject later on. What received too little attention, as we can see in retrospect, was the need to establish a just political order internally within Iraq as a key part of securing peace in the Gulf region. Given the focus of international law on affairs *between* nations, however, and the reluctance of the international community (including the coalition partners) to interfere in the internal affairs of nations, it is understandable that the coalition confined its conception of post-crisis peace to the restoration of order among the affected nations. The broader just war tradition differs from international law on this matter of whether the use of force to achieve peace should extend to efforts to produce the conditions of peace within the offending state; the moral argument imposes a more extensive responsibility than the legal.

(It is worth noting that many of those who insist that modern war is inherently immoral define "peace" as no-resort-to-military-force at all, and make this the first goal of international politics. Though these critics may use just war terminology to argue their case, their argument is fundamentally at odds with the central assumption in just war tradition: that there may be criminal acts against order and justice in the relations among nations and peoples, and that force may be the only way to achieve a stable condition of justice and peacefulness.)

Proportionality of Good Over Evil

The next just war concept to be examined is the criterion of *proportionality*, which refers to the effort to calculate the overall balance of good versus evil in deciding whether to use force to right a wrong. One must first assess the evil that has already been done—damage to lives and property, as well as harm to the more intangible values of human rights, self-government, and a peaceful and stable world order. Second, one must calculate the costs of allowing the situation of wrongdoing to continue. Finally, one must evaluate the various means of righting these wrongs in terms of their own costs, as well as the benefits they might produce.

In the debate that took place over U.S. participation in the United Nations–sanctioned use of force against Iraq, the just war criterion of proportionality was widely misapplied. Critics of the use of force vastly overestimated the expected costs of war while paying little attention to the damage already done, and continuing to be done, by Iraq's aggression against Kuwait.[34] For these critics, the moral problem was not Iraq's actions but the American military buildup, which they deemed "disproportionate." The decision whether to take military action requires a much more inclusive and objective weighing of good versus ill.

The calculation of proportionality must take into account the many levels of force that responsible leaders may choose. While there may be occasions in which a buildup would serve as an effective deterrent, there are numerous other ways of engaging in combat, each carrying its own costs and benefits.

Applying the criterion of proportionality is properly an exercise in moral and political judgment, not a mathematical calculation. While it is easy to count military personnel, tanks, airplanes, and munitions, it is more difficult to agree on the value that should be placed on protection of human rights, national territorial and governmental integrity, and other such intangibles. Yet these are among the paramount values the just war tradition seeks to preserve, and their importance is undeniable. Equally undeniable is the fact that different peoples and cultures place different stock in these values. For this reason, governments need to take special care when invoking considerations of proportionality to keep from conceiving the issue in narrowly political or cultural terms.

Reasonable Hope of Success

The decision to resort to force, to be justified, must also rest on a conviction that military action will have a *reasonable hope of success*. Clearly this, too, is a matter for prudential judgment, since "success" can be interpreted in many ways. While the fundamental goal of just war tradition is the protection and preservation of values—specifically, the establishment of right order, justice, and peace, within this broad context any particular just use of force may have its own specific aims. Indeed, such aims are inherently narrower than the overarching goal of right politics, a goal that is achieved by many instruments, only one of which is the justified use of force.

The use of force may establish the *conditions* for order, justice, and peace by eliminating the threats posed to them; that is the most realistic definition of "success" in the use of military force. The actual *achievement* of these goals is the broader work of good statecraft, building on the base of the established conditions. Clausewitz's famous dictum, "War is the continuation of politics by other means," has a corollary: it is the business of politics to build on what a just war makes possible. A justified resort to force will have a "reasonable hope of success" if it lays the groundwork for productive statecraft (or, at the minimum, does not foster a situation that might make such statecraft impossible).

It is inappropriate to demand that a just use of force achieve ends beyond its means. This is why, in both classic and contemporary just war reasoning, the idea of specific and limited war goals is central. It is also why just war tradition developed a *ius in bello*, a set of restraints on what may morally be done when fighting a justified war. The concept of *ius in bello* involves more than insuring that the means of war are justifiable in themselves; it also involves establishing a correct relationship between the belligerents, both during the war and afterwards, since it recognizes that the existence of such a relationship is an important precondition for the creation of a just and lasting peace. "Reasonable hope of success," then, turns on the understanding of just cause and right intention, and includes not only achieving the goals thus established but also observing the limits on means laid out in the *ius in bello*. What is called for, in short, is a reasonable hope of doing what is justified by these moral criteria within the moral limits they define.

War as Last Resort

Finally, before engaging in military action, a government should determine whether the wrongs involved can be redressed by means other than force. It is important to note that the criterion of last resort does not mean that all possible nonmilitary options that may be conceived of must first be tried; rather, a prudential judgment must be made as to whether *only* a rightly authorized use of force can, in the given circumstances, achieve the goods defined by the ideas of just cause, right intention, and the goal of peace, at a proportionate cost, and with reasonable hope of success. Other methods *may* be tried first, if time permits and if they also satisfy these moral criteria; yet this is not mandated by the criterion of last resort —and "last resort" certainly does not mean that other methods must be tried indefinitely.

THE CASE OF IRAQ

It is my judgment that all the just war criteria providing guidance on the justified use of force were amply satisfied in the case of the decision to use military force against Iraq. The decision not to continue with negotiations or economic sanctions after January 15, 1991, did not violate the criterion of "last resort." The failure of the Geneva talks, the continued intransigence of Saddam Hussein, the ongoing process of military buildup by Iraqi forces, the continuing systematic rape of Kuwait, the history of Iraq's relations with its own dissident population and its neighbors, and threats of violence by Iraq against those neighbors all provided ample reasons to conclude that non-military means held little possibility of success, and that the continuing atrocities in Kuwait necessitated action.

Indeed, Iraq was an easy case. Most instances are fraught with much more ambiguity. There was no moral equivalence between Iraq and Kuwait, for example, or between Iraq and the coalition nations. Iraq's actions flagrantly violated both international law and the deeper international conscience expressed in the idea of a peaceful and stable world order. Nor were military forces committed by the United States or the other coalition nations behind closed doors; the authorization was public, was worked out in debate, and, when it came, clearly represented the will of the authorizing bodies. The critics' charges of a hidden American agenda were not borne out, either during or after the fact. The use of force was proportionate, given the wrongs that were to be righted. The continual aggression on the part of Saddam Hussein swept away, one by one, other possible means of resolving the crisis short of force. The judgment of a reasonable hope of success was eminently sound. The coalition's military action was motivated by the desire to lay a foundation for peace. While the final establishment of peace in the Gulf region and throughout the Middle East clearly remains to be accomplished, that is the proper task for statecraft, and exceeds the bounds of what military force alone can ever achieve.

Moral Limits on the Use of Force

We turn now to the other side of just war tradition, the moral limitations on justified force: the *ius in bello*. Once the decision is made that force is justified, just war tradition sets two conditions on how that force may be employed: noncombatants must be protected from direct, intentional attack (the principle of *discrimination*), and the specific means of force must be at a level and of a type appropriate to the task at hand (the principle of *proportionality of means*).

The question of proportionality in combat is similar to the concept of proportionality in deciding whether to resort to force. But in this instance, the calculus of "proportion" hinges more narrowly on the legitimate military goals to be achieved, the forces arrayed on the enemy side, and the least destructive ways to defeat those forces or render them ineffective so as to achieve those legitimate ends. Proportionality is not concerned with the absolute quantities of personnel or weaponry employed, but with their relationship to the existing threat and with their effect. In the case of the Gulf War, the flanking maneuver by which Operation Desert Storm achieved its swift victory displayed a clear case of proportionality of means as opposed to choosing a frontal assault on Iraqi fortifications. Proportionality was evident not only in the low casualties to coalition forces, but also in the relatively low casualties to Iraqi forces, testified to by the large numbers of prisoners of war taken by the coalition.

The principle of discrimination requires that noncombatants should not be directly, intentionally targeted, even in the course of using force that is otherwise proportionate. It is morally meaningful—and empirically possible—to distinguish noncombatants from combatants: the former have no direct material or formal participation in the war, while the latter do. Means of warfare that cannot make this distinction are morally wrong, such as the use of poison gas against civilian populations in an attempt to suppress dissidence, or counter-population bombing in an effort to undermine civilian morale. By contrast, means of warfare that directly, intentionally strike at legitimate military targets—including deployments of troops, munitions depots, weapons-production facilities, and command-and-control centers—are morally and legally permissible, even if noncombatant lives and property are inadvertently put at risk or damaged.

The Challenge of Modern Warfare

Since the 1950s many have argued that contemporary war is inherently indiscriminate and disproportionate. In support of their view, they invoke World War II, the Vietnam War, and, perhaps most prominently, the possibility of a nuclear holocaust. Others have countered that since 1945 warfare has been of a far less deadly variety than World War II, consisting primarily of local conflicts; furthermore these conflicts have, with the exception of the use of chemical weapons in the Iraq-Iran war, relied on conventional weaponry.

The experience of such wars shows that, while individual leaders may wrongly choose to ignore the combatant–noncombatant distinction, it is by no means the case that "modern warfare" has made this distinction any more difficult. Some, including myself, have stressed that the presence or absence of discrimination in war is not a function of the destructive capabilities of the weapons available but a direct product of the intentions of those who employ them. A corollary to this observation is that the destructive capabilities of modern weaponry—conventional as well as nuclear, chemical, or biological—morally require parallel developments designed to limit the collateral damage of weapons, to increase their accuracy, and to create tactical and strategic plans that would ensure that such means of war are used in accordance with the principles of discrimination and proportionality.

The Gulf War clearly showed that contemporary warfare may in fact be conducted within the limits imposed by these two just war principles; at the same time, it showed that doing so—as well as *preparing* to do so—is still a matter of moral or immoral choice, just as it was in previous ages. "Smart" bombs, highly accurate cruise missiles, even the latest in aiming devices for "dumb" bombs and missiles, as well as intelligence-gathering means that can identify and pinpoint specific buildings as military targets—all these means of war employed by the coalition forces stand in stark distinction to the bombing and shelling practices of World War II and even Vietnam. Critics of the U.S. role in the Gulf War remarked that the great majority of munitions dropped in the air war were not of these high-accuracy types. That charge misses two important points: first, that high-technology weaponry, with its increased ability to satisfy the requirements of discrimination and proportionality, has made possible a very different sort of "contemporary war" than these critics have imagined; second, that even the routine weapons used in the air war did not violate acceptable means of war. The United States did not use such weapons with indiscriminate or murderous intent, and there is evidence that U.S. military leaders deliberately rejected the option of intentional counter-population bombing, as when swift action was taken against Air Force General Michael Dugan in September 1990 when he suggested employing such a tactic against Baghdad.[35]

In contrast, Iraq's conduct of war was in conspicuous violation of the principles of discrimination and proportion. It is important to remember that these principles, like other ideas embodied in just war tradition, are not simply part of the moral heritage of the West; they are present also in Islamic moral tradition, and they are explicitly part of international law. The immoral and illegal warfare tactics employed by Iraq included the conscious use of counter-population targeting of Kuwaiti citizens and others trapped by the invasion, both at the beginning and throughout the occupation; the launching of Scud missiles against Saudi and Israeli cities in direct, intentional counter-population strikes; the loosing of oil into the Persian Gulf in an effort to impede coalition sea and amphibious action; and, at the time of the withdrawal of Iraqi forces, their destruction of Kuwaiti buildings, systematic pillaging of Kuwaiti property, and setting afire Kuwaiti oil wells and facilities. Most of these acts had no military relevance whatsoever, and the damage they created will continue to cause widespread harm for years to come. Such long-term damage is inherently indiscriminate, for, as we have already noted, once a war is over all are noncombatants.

Persistent Misconceptions About War

As I have suggested above, thinking about the "last" war (whether World War II or Vietnam) has deeply affected American moral debate over military matters. The World War II countercity bombing of German and Japanese cities furnished models for both sides of the debate over nuclear targeting and deterrence strategy. On the one hand, proponents of strategic nuclear targeting of Soviet cities in the 1950s found their rationale in the countercity bombing that took place during World War II. On the other hand, opponents of nuclear-weapons strategy took their bearings from this same model, viewing modern war as inevitably all-encompassing in scope and indiscriminate in targets. Both sides, then, for very different reasons, found themselves in agreement that "in modern wars there are no noncombatants." Paul Ramsey's effort to assert the just war principle of discrimination, first set out in *War and the Christian Conscience*, was a notable exception in the debate, arguing that, even in modern wars, the distinction between combatants and noncombatants can and must be observed. Unfortunately, the American experience in Vietnam, with its high casualties and the close relation of guerrillas and their civilian supporters, further strengthened the claim that modern wars are inherently indiscriminate and disproportionate. Opponents of the Vietnam War in particular represented it as typical of war in the modern age and used it to argue against use of military force in general.

Imagining War in the Gulf

In the debate over American military involvement in the Gulf crisis much opposition centered on judgments based on this understanding of modern war. Critics feared the war would unleash a holocaust of destruction, and this fear in turn fueled arguments that U.S. deployment of force was disproportionate, that the use in combat of this force would be disproportionate and indiscriminate, and therefore that force should not be employed. The myth of war inherited from the "last" wars thus skewed moral judgments about the rightness of force in this crisis.

The Gulf War, on the contrary, showed that it is possible to fight a contemporary war within the bounds of the just war principles of discrimination and proportionality of means, and that the decision to do so is a moral judgment on the part of the belligerents involved, not a choice forced on them by contemporary weapons. There is, I think, a lesson to be drawn from this: we need to put aside our fears that contemporary war must, by its very nature, be an indiscriminate, disproportionate holocaust, and move on to deliberate the best ways of developing means of force that may be used morally if military action is necessary. In contrast to the destructiveness exemplified in World War II's carpet-bombing of cities and Vietnam's free-fire zones, the Gulf War showed that highly accurate weapons and appropriate plans and policies for their use can limit the overall destructiveness of contemporary war. The Gulf War, in short, is a real-life example of what just war tradition has always held to be true in principle: war is an enterprise capable of being conducted morally or immorally, depending on human decisions.

The Value of Ius ad Bellum

An important implication of the conduct of the Gulf War for the American moral debate on military matters is that we ought now to be able to concentrate on judging the rightness or wrongness of particular possible uses of force in terms of the *ius ad bellum* categories—just cause, right authority, right intention, and so on—instead of falling into the tendency to reason backwards from judgments about whether *ius in bello* could be observed. If war itself is recognized as subject to human control, and if the means of war are also known to be subject to such control, then the logic of just war tradition is restored: that, first, a decision must be made as to whether a resort to force is justifiable in itself; second, decisions must be made as to how to employ that force in justifiable ways.

These assumptions also carry important implications for the development of American military capabilities. We seem to have moved into a cycle of limited warfare, having passed through a period of world-wide conflicts. Whether this is a genuine cycle or not, or whether total war and limited war are always parallel options, we would do well to note William V. O'Brien's observation that limited war represents the practical application of the just war idea.[36] Whereas the Cold War, as well as the models of the two World Wars, encouraged those engaged in the moral debate to focus on an image of total war, the Gulf War provides a powerful historical example to buttress the moral argument for military preparedness oriented to limited and humanly controllable forms of warfare.

The Goal of Peace

The earliest modern visions of structures of international cooperation, those of seventeenth- and eighteenth-century theorists like Crucé, Sully, Saint-Pierre, Penn, and Bentham, aimed at producing what Saint-Pierre called "perpetual peace" and what Kant similarly termed "eternal peace."[37] Such is the heritage of international organizations like the League of Nations and the United Nations. But this is also the heritage of regional forms of cooperative relationship set up to enable states to settle their differences constructively and to manage their common affairs for mutual benefit. The goal of international order is the goal of a just and enduring peace.

Just war tradition specifies that a justified resort to force in international disputes must aim at producing peace. More broadly, as I have argued above, the tradition understands this peace as one that flows from and accompanies the establishment of a right political order and justice within and among nations.

International law, which is one of the most important carriers of just war tradition in the contemporary world, defines order, justice, and peace in relatively straightforward terms: order is the recognition of the integrity of states; justice is the provision for recognition of states and formal equality of treatment within a legal community of nations, the United Nations; peace is the state of affairs in which order and justice, thus defined, coexist (or, more narrowly, when no nation or group of nations is threatening another nation or group of nations so as to deny them national rights or political, territorial, or economic integrity). Working from this standard, the U.N. Security Council authorized the use of force to expel Iraq from Kuwait and to restore Kuwaiti territory and national autonomy. The goal was, as much as possible, to restore the *status quo ante bellum*.

A New World Order?

Beyond the scope of international law, however, matters are more complicated. President Bush, in justifying the war, called for a "new world order." Critics of the war argued that it would inflame the entire region, ending whatever stability and limited peace had been achieved there. Thus, both agreed that forcing Iraq out of Kuwait would be only a stepping-stone to peace; the coalition victory, as well as the manner in which it was achieved, would have to set in motion a general reordering of relations among the nations of the region so as to bring about a more general, pervasive, and enduring state of peace. In particular, such a peace would need to include a new mutual security arrangement for the Gulf region itself, replacing the old tripartite balancing of power by Iran, Iraq, and Saudi Arabia, and a settlement of the conflict between Israel and the Arab states.

Obstacles to Peace

Both of these goals will clearly be difficult to achieve and will require intensive efforts well beyond the immediate accomplishments of the Gulf War.

Media attention, meanwhile, has focused on the mix of promise and challenges in the relationship between Israel and its Arab adversaries. There are indeed difficulties aplenty here, and while there is much optimism that they can be overcome, the war against Iraq in fact had little directly to do with the core issues: the right of Israel to exist as a state and the solution of the Palestinian problem. What the war did perhaps create is a new network of relationships that may allow for more productive and trusting interaction among some of the actors in the Israeli-Arab conflict. This will not be easy, given that the Palestinians were on the other side in the war, and that many of them in Jordan long remained captive to the view that Saddam Hussein's forces won. (Indeed, in the summer of 1991, postwar Iraqi propaganda continued to represent Saddam Hussein as having achieved a great victory by successfully resisting Western and Zionist imperialism.)[38]

The Syrians have their own political goals that may or may not in the long term be compatible with making peace with Israel. The Saudis continue to have their own regional agenda, and are hamstrung as well at crucial points by a religious conservatism that dictates implacable hostility to Israel; while they will no longer dispense great sums of money to the PLO, Jordan, and Iraq, there are no signs that the Saudi government will go beyond a de facto neutrality regarding Israel—if they even go that far. As for the Israelis, the war has left them strategically much stronger in the region, and their internal political situation makes them unlikely to accept a compromise involving "land for peace." Again, the chances are not great that the Gulf War will produce a "new world order" in the Israeli-Arab conflict.

A new mutual security arrangement in the Gulf area is more possible, yet still fraught with problems. Fixated by the seemingly intractable problem of an Israeli-Arab peace, Americans have paid far less attention to the broader issues of regional security than those issues deserve. Saddam Hussein's continued grasp on the Iraqi state and use of the machinery of absolute rule against his country's population is a major barrier to progress in settling the larger problem of the future role of Iraq in the region. If there is ever to be a lasting peace in the area, it must be preceded by the rebuilding of Iraq, the creation of some form of democratic self-government there, and the inculcation of values oriented toward peaceful coexistence with its neighbor states. Saddam Hussein's military forces caused great and unwonted destruction to Kuwait and its people; yet Iraq itself—its people, its cities, and its land—has also experienced much destruction, as a result both of the war and of subsequent Iraqi military actions against the Kurds and the Shi'ites. The achievement of a just and enduring peace rests on remedying this situation.

Achieving this goal will be no easy matter, given the vitriolic animosity Saddam Hussein's aggressive actions have aroused in most of his neighbors, including the most powerful ones. Enduring peace will be impossible to achieve if Saddam Hussein remains at the head of the Iraqi state. Equally important, the United States must take the same leadership role in working toward the political reconstruction of Iraq and the region that it took in the fight against Iraq—or, for that matter, in the reconstruction of West Germany and Japan after 1945. This implies a new commitment to the support of human rights in the region and the protection of oppressed minorities, such as the Kurds.

America as a Moral Agent

The reluctance of the United States to assume a more active role stems largely from its desire to stay within the bounds of what is allowed by international law in rolling back aggression. But the end result may be that the only peace that can be achieved in this region is one limited to that defined by international law, not a "new order" that will be extraordinarily difficult to bring into being.

This is not to minimize some of the accomplishments of the *old* order. Restoring the territorial integrity and governmental autonomy of Kuwait, reestablishing respect for the anti-aggression rule of international law, restoring credibility to the moral and legal guidelines for resort to force and for fighting justly, restoring to the United Nations the ability to act in the world as its designers intended—these are goals deeply worthy in themselves and fundamental to the preservation of international peace. As always, peace is not something to be set in place and then walked away from; it requires constant tending and reconstruction. The outcome of the Gulf War may not be the ideal peace that everyone longs for. But the war has produced a peace that is surely preferable to the appeasement urged by some in the fall of 1990, and it has strengthened the tools for preserving a minimum of the peace of order among nations.

What should be the role of the United States in the evolving international order? America today stands in a position of unrivaled strength among world powers, and it is clearly the object of much envy on the part of people around the world. While no country can single-handedly deal with all the world's problems, the leadership role the United States has assumed in the Middle East since August 2, 1990, suggests that Americans might now do a great deal more in the international arena than was conceivable so long as the Cold War lasted. American leadership might be exercised through the United Nations, whose Security Council functioned in the Gulf crisis as it was designed to function but had not since 1945; American leadership might be exercised through alliances or coalitions of nations dealing with regional problems; or, on rare occasions, America may need to exercise its influence alone.

Using influence does not necessarily mean taking military action, although as Paul Ramsey argued in a passage quoted earlier, the exercise of statecraft inevitably involves the use of national power, and the military represents a component of such power. Thus it is important to keep the just war debate alive in this post–Gulf War era, for its categories may need to be drawn on again in assessing our proper response to crises that may erupt in the future. As the Gulf crisis has shown, it is also important to think of the contemporary meaning of this moral tradition not simply in terms of the debate over nuclear weapons and deterrence, which preoccupied just war theorists for most of three decades from 1945 until the end of the Cold War, but also in terms of weapons-planning and development, strategic and tactical thought, and the socialization and training of military personnel. In short, it is time to rethink our moral tradition of statecraft and force it back to its roots, and to reconsider the tradition's implications for present and future policy, anticipating an active American role in the developing world order that lies ahead.

Part Two

The Churches and the Gulf Crisis

War, Peace, and the Christian Conscience

George Weigel

AMERICA, as Chesterton famously said, is "a nation with the soul of a church." That being the case, America's religious institutions—its churches, synagogues, mosques, as well as its ecumenical and inter-religious agencies—play a role in the public policy debate that is without parallel in other advanced industrialized nations. The public debates that took place in the latter half of 1990 over operations Desert Shield and Desert Storm are the latest illustrations of this striking phenomenon.

To be sure, America's religious institutions shape public moral argument in many different ways, and at different levels of influence. The culture-shaping and norm-defining churches of the once-great liberal Protestant mainline—Episcopal, Congregational, Presbyterian, Methodist—have been in something of a demographic free-fall since the Second World War. This numerical decline (the equivalent, it was once calculated, of the loss of a seven-hundred-member congregation on every day since V-J Day) has been paralleled by a dramatic radicalization of the social witness of these churches. To take but one symbolic reference point: with Edmond Lee Browning as its presiding bishop, the Episcopal Church can hardly be called "the Republican Party at prayer."[1]

During the same post-war period, Roman Catholicism in America has grown in both numbers and influence. Catholicism is now the largest voluntary association in the United States, with Catholics making up over 25 percent of the national population. The Church's membership is now largely middle- and upper-middle class, and thus in a more advantageous position to bring its leverage to bear on public moral argument than was the case when American Catholicism was very much an immigrant church. The Catholic bishops of the United States have become increasingly vocal participants in the public policy debate, on matters ranging from abortion to nuclear weapons. And the century-old tradition of modern Catholic social thought has been expanded and developed in a distinctively American fashion by Catholic philosophers, theologians, and political theorists of many theological and political persuasions.[2]

The post-war period has also witnessed, along with the decline of the old Protestant mainline, a demographic, intellectual, and political renaissance among conservative or evangelical Protestants. This striking development has not been so unilinear in its impact on public life as one would gather from the often-fevered press coverage of the religious new right. For while it is true that evangelical Protestants have tended to match their conservative theology with a politics that is more conservative than that espoused by their liberal mainline brethren, the evangelical world has also given birth over the past generation to new forms of Christian radicalism that marry literalist readings of the Old and New Testaments to the politics of the Sixties in a distinctive, and sometimes volatile, mix.[3]

Throughout this same period, of course, American Jewish leaders and American Jewish organizations have been active and influential on a host of public policy issues ranging from civil rights to questions of the First Amendment religious liberty clause to grave matters of America's role in world politics.

In short, the question in America is not *whether* religious institutions and their moral arguments are going to shape the debate over the future of the American experiment and its relationship to the world, but the degree of moral wisdom they bring to the debate. Will America's religious institutions help nurture and deepen genuinely public moral argument, or will they simply advance preconceived political—indeed, partisan—agendas dressed up in the language of morality and religious conviction?

Unhappily, it cannot be said that the formal leadership of the American religious community brought very much wisdom on matters of ethics and international affairs to the debate before, during, and after the Persian Gulf war. The two key sectors of the American religious community in this debate—and the sectors which disappointed, although in different degrees—were mainline Protestantism and its ecumenical agency, the National Council of the Churches of Christ in the U.S.A. (NCC), and the Roman Catholic Church, through the National Conference of Catholic Bishops (NCCB) and its public policy agency, the United States Catholic Conference (USCC).

Evangelical Protestantism played a far less visible role in the Gulf debate than had been the case on any number of hotly contested issues in the 1980s. Prominent individual evangelical leaders—among them the dean of evangelical social ethicists, Carl F. H. Henry, and the Rev. Jerry Falwell—did give public support to Bush administration policy. And in what was perhaps an important augury of the future, Richard Land, president of the Christian Life Commission of the rapidly growing and increasingly powerful Southern Baptist Convention, analyzed the question of a possible U.S. military involvement in the Gulf crisis through the moral canons of the just war tradition, a tradition of moral reasoning whose "location" in American religion is usually considered to be in the Roman Catholic Church and in those dwindling sectors of liberal

Protestantism influenced by the work of the late Paul Ramsey.[4] These were not insignificant interventions in the debate. But the fact remains that the most prominent evangelical voice in the Gulf argument, as we will discuss below, was that of Jim Wallis, who hails from the far larboard borderlands of political evangelicaldom.

Nor did the American Jewish community, whose chief organizations were generally supportive of Bush administration policy, shape the public moral argument over the Gulf crisis in any significant way; and this despite the fact that the Gulf War became the occasion for some striking soul-searching among prominent intellectuals on the American Jewish Left.[5]

In sum, the most visible and influential religious actors in the Gulf debate were the mainline Protestant churches and the National Council of Churches, and the Catholic bishops. Analyzing the themes of these churches' address to the Gulf crisis, and scouting the terrain for the future of the religiously grounded moral argument over America's right role in the world, therefore requires that primary attention be paid to these churches and their leaders. Thus this essay examines, first, the mainline Protestant, NCC, and Roman Catholic contributions to the American debate between August 2, 1990 (when Iraq invaded Kuwait), and January 16, 1991 (when Operation Desert Storm began). The second part of the essay will suggest how the churches might have been wiser moral counsellors to the American body politic, and will explore several issues whose resolution will largely determine whether the churches will bring more light than heat to similar debates in the future.

The Debate Before Desert Storm

About the public debate preceding Operation Desert Storm, two things may be said with some confidence.

First, there has rarely been such a sustained (and in many

respects, impressive) public grappling with the moral criteria and political logic of the just war tradition. Administration officials, members of Congress, senior military officers, columnists, talk-show hosts, and ordinary citizens debated the goals and instruments of U.S. Gulf policy in such classic just war terms as "just cause," "competent authority," "probability of success," "last resort," "proportionality" (of ends, and of means to ends), and "discrimination" (between combatants and noncombatants). Nor did the public debate restrict itself to these familiar criteria of the *ius ad bellum* (what William V. O'Brien once called "war-decision law") and the *ius in bello* (O'Brien's "war-conduct law"). Viewed from one angle, the entire debate was also an attempt to clarify the key issues of the *ius ad pacem* that is contained in the intellectual trajectory and interstices of the just war tradition: What kind of peace can be sought in this world? How, and under what political and military circumstances, can the proportionate and discriminate use of armed force serve the ends of peace, which include security, freedom, justice, and order?

Those who listened carefully to this five-month-long public argument could hear, woven through it, the conviction that "war" and "peace" do not exist in hermetically sealed compartments but are parts of a single human universe of moral discourse, a universe that is at one and the same time "political" and "moral." It was a heartening debate for those concerned with the health of public moral discourse in the United States, and for those who had long argued that the just war tradition was alive and well in the American body politic.

The second truth about the debate is, as suggested above, a far less happy one. At the very time that America was engaged in a profound moral argument about its use of power in the world—indeed, in a profound moral argument about the shape of world politics in the post–Cold War world—much of the formal religious leadership of the country, and particularly the leadership of mainline/oldline Protestantism and the

Roman Catholic Church, abdicated its teaching responsibilities and showed itself incapable of providing the kind of public moral leadership it had traditionally exercised in American society.

The Abandonment of Christian Realism

One can go even further. The debate over the Gulf crisis marked the point at which the Christian Realism expounded by Reinhold Niebuhr and the aforementioned Paul Ramsey was definitively abandoned by the mainline/oldline leadership and the National Council of Churches. And in its place was substituted a curdled hash composed in part of unvarnished *Tercermundismo* and in part of a neo-isolationist version of precisely that liberal Protestant sentimentality against which Niebuhr and Ramsey had inveighed: now, it appears, to little effect, insofar as the mainline/oldline leadership is concerned.

But in the circumstances in which one expects they are now resident, Niebuhr and Ramsey were quite probably not alone in wondering what in the world (so to speak) was going on. For their Catholic analogue, John Courtney Murray, could take little satisfaction from the performance of the episcopal leaders of American Catholicism who, during the Gulf crisis, did little to vindicate Murray's claim that theirs were the hands into which the faltering torch of Christian Realism would be passed.

To be sure, the religious debate over the Gulf crisis had its amusing moments, if one's sense of humor is sufficiently spiced with a sense of irony. *Sojourners*, scourge of American capitalism and the flagship magazine of *soi-disant* "radical biblical Christianity," made the Gulf debate the occasion for some opportunistic fundraising. "Many peace and justice organizations have experienced lean times lately with the ending of the Cold War," according to *Sojourners*. "The war fever in the Persian Gulf demonstrates that, unfortunately, peacemaking will never be out of style. Send a check today!"

Not to be outdone in the category of general tawdriness was "Network," the self-styled "national Catholic social justice lobby" whose coordinator, Sister Nancy Sylvester, began a fundraising letter in these lurid terms: "Dear Friend, As I write this letter, war in the Persian Gulf threatens to tear our world apart . . ."—which evil happenstance could, evidently, be avoided by joining Sister Nancy's lobbying organization and supporting its work "for a fundamental re-ordering of our national priorities." It hardly needs be added that the organization's sense of our "national priorities" is indistinguishable from that of the Rainbow Coalition.

But this was mere froth on the kettle. What was churning in the pot was a host of dubious moral and political assumptions that had, over the past twenty-five years, achieved a kind of *de fide* status in the mainline/oldline and in a considerable segment of the Catholic leadership. A review of the literature suggests just what those assumptions were, and illustrates the extraordinary grip they have on the religious leaders who, against virtually all the empirical evidence, continue to proclaim them as something approaching self-evident truths.

The NCC Strikes Back

For an organization like the National Council of Churches, whose pitiful recent decline was described by its former general secretary as a passage from the mainline to the oldline to the sideline, the Gulf crisis may have seemed a godsend. Here at last was the opportunity to recoup the losses of the past generation and to regain the leadership position that had been severely eroded by years of demographic decline, financial mismanagement, and the dramatic falsification of the NCC worldview by the Revolution of 1989, the ouster of the Sandinistas in Nicaragua, and the democratic/capitalist revolution that seemed to be sweeping the world. Attention, it must have seemed, would be paid: as indeed it was, by journalists who were either too ignorant or too committed to the NCC's politics to challenge its spurious claim that the Council represented some 42 million Americans (fully 65 percent of whom, it can be safely assumed, rejected the NCC's political stance on the Gulf).

Blaming America First—Again

But in fact what the NCC demonstrated, in a veritable blizzard of "messages," "resolutions," and faxes to the president, and in a highly publicized "Church Leaders' Peace Pilgrimage to the Middle East" (staged just before Christmas, on December 14–21, 1990), was how utterly beholden it remained to the politics of blaming America first, and how little it had to offer to serious moral debate about the ends and means of U.S. policy in the Persian Gulf.

As early as September 14, 1990, the NCC's Executive Coordinating Committee was critical of the deployment of U.S. forces to the Gulf, an action that, according to the NCC, raised the specter of "Vietnam."[6] The Executive Coordinating Committee did condemn the Iraqi invasion and occupation of Kuwait, and applauded the way in which the Bush administration had used the United Nations. But the gravamen of the NCC's concerns, at this early date, clearly had to do with the possible use of American military power in the Gulf—a point that was driven home in no uncertain terms two months later, when the General Board of the NCC adopted a "Message on the Gulf and Middle East Crisis" that fairly bristled with resentment over the continued buildup of U.S. forces in the Gulf. The Bush administration, according to the "message," was guilty of "reckless rhetoric" and "imprudent behavior" that had led to "widespread speculation in our country, in the Middle East, and elsewhere that the United States will initiate war." In the face of such provocations, the NCC felt compelled to "unequivocally . . . oppose actions that could have such dire consequences."

But the NCC was not content with warnings against the "militarization" of the conflict. The itch to play geopolitician proving irresistible, the NCC went on to urge effective linkage between the Iraqi occupation of Kuwait and Israel's position in the occupied territories (which, it will be remembered, was precisely Saddam Hussein's proposal at the time). Indeed, if one extrapolated Saddam Hussein's intentions from the NCC's descriptions of the realities of the Middle East, the Iraqi dictator invaded and occupied Kuwait in order to help the Palestinians—a proposition that would have been risible if it were not so desperately and tragically wrong-headed.[7]

A Morally Impoverished Argument

The November 15 "message" of the NCC concluded by making a dichotomy between "a new era of international cooperation under the rule of law" and "rule based upon superior power" (as if the rule of law in international affairs could be enforced by good will alone). But, its political foolishness aside, what was so striking about the NCC "message" was its sheer poverty as a moral reflection. The document contained two brief biblical citations, and its opening section carried the headline: "Theological and Moral Imperatives." But there was no theology here, in any recognizable sense of the term. Just war criteria—as principles of statecraft, and as criteria for assessing the morality of the possible use of armed force in the Gulf—were singularly and glaringly absent from the NCC's document.

But neither was the NCC "message" rooted in principled pacifism. It simply lacked any serious moral content at all, substituting for moral analysis a tendentious and myopic reading of Middle Eastern politics, coupled with the hoary charge that it was American power that was most to be feared in the region. (Even this failed to satisfy United Methodist Bishop Melvin Talbert of San Francisco, chairman of the NCC committee that drafted the resolution accompanying the November 15 "message," who urged his fellow bishops in California and Nevada to speak out against "U.S. aggression in the region." President Bush, according to Talbert, was the "real aggressor" in the Gulf, and represented an America that hadn't "learned anything from Vietnam and Korea."[8])

A month later, in the week before Christmas, the NCC's staff coordinated a widely publicized "Church Leaders' Peace Pilgrimage to the Middle East." The message "to the American people" released by the eighteen oldline and Orthodox leaders who participated in this classic political pilgrimage ratcheted up the rhetoric of the November 15 NCC "message" more than a few notches. The resort to armed force by the United States "would be politically and morally indefensible." (Note the sequence of concerns.) "It is entirely possible that war in the Middle East will destroy everything." (Everything?) The "war option" would yield "certain catastrophe." (The "peace pilgrims" couldn't even get the basic facts straight: according to their message, Jordan was led by a "compassionate" and "democratic" government.)

And the alternative to the "war option"? It lay, according to the pilgrims, in "citizen action and the strength of public opinion," which could "literally make possible a solution to this crisis without war." *How* was not specified.[9]

The Implications of Isolationism

One cannot know with certainty the motivations of the denominational leaders and others who participated in this alleged peace pilgrimage. But what can be said with assurance is that its effect, given the post-pilgrimage message and what it reveals about the politics of those involved, was to reinforce Saddam Hussein's view that the force of public opinion could be used to compel the United States and its allies to stand down from their commitments to Iraq's unconditional withdrawal from Kuwait. The "Church Leaders' Peace Pilgrimage" was, in short, nothing of the sort. It was, rather, a grotesquely irresponsible action that arguably made a military confrontation more likely in the Gulf.

Finally, on January 15, 1991, the day U.N. resolutions had specified as the absolute deadline for Iraqi withdrawal from Kuwait, the NCC coordinated a fax letter to President Bush from thirty-two heads of denominations and ecumenical organizations that urged the president, "Do not lead our nation into this abyss," for, once begun, "it is unlikely that this battle can be contained in either scope, intensity, or time." Moreover, the "sacrifice" Bush seemed prepared to make "is out of proportion to any conceivable gain which might be achieved through military action."[10]

No parallel request was made to Saddam Hussein, urging him to comply with the relevant U.N. resolutions. Indeed, throughout the five-and-a-half months of the Gulf debate, between the invasion of Kuwait and the launching of Operation Desert Storm, the NCC was immeasurably more concerned about the possibility of the use of U.S. military force in the Persian Gulf than it was about resisting the aggression of Saddam Hussein.

"War" would begin, and "peace" would end, when U.S. forces were engaged; it did not seem to occur to the officials of the NCC, and to the mainline/oldline denominational heads who aligned themselves with the NCC, that war had begun on August 2, 1990, with the Iraqi invasion of Kuwait. There was no "peace" in the Persian Gulf after August 2; but one would never have learned that from the NCC.

A Double Standard of Condemnation

Especially striking for an organization that has not been loath to condemn human rights violations committed by regimes it regards with disfavor, the NCC was silent about the post-invasion rape of Kuwait, which included (according to an Amnesty International report released in December 1990) such refinements of social control as the bayonetting of pregnant women, the summary execution of children in front of their parents, and the abandonment to their deaths of infants torn from their hospital incubators. Nary a rubber bullet can be fired on the West Bank or in Gaza without engaging the wrath of the NCC. But about the rape of Kuwait, a gruesome and odious business even by the debased standards of the neighborhood, the NCC was virtually silent.

Such moral obtuseness was of a piece with the NCC's puerile analysis of the politics of the Middle East. Time and again the NCC warned, between August 1990 and January 1991, that any U.S. military action would inevitably inflame the Arab masses, would revive ancient cultural phobias about Western crusaders, and would yield an unbridgeable chasm between the United States and the Arab countries.

Indeed, so deeply had the NCC drunk from this particular well of disinformation that it seemingly could not grasp the most elementary facts: that Saddam had in fact invaded another Arab country; that leading Arab powers such as Egypt and Saudi Arabia were allies of the United States, and moreover allies who seemed eager for Saddam and his regime to be disposed of; that Saddam's Arab support, such as it was, came from such poor fish as Yemen, the PLO, and Libya. No, in the NCC's view of the world, it was "the Arabs against the United States"—which was, of course, precisely the view of the matter that Saddam Hussein was busily promoting. Nor did the NCC make any effort to distinguish its reading of the realities from Saddam's.[11]

For decades now, the National Council of Churches has urged that the United Nations be more regularly and effectively used as an instrument for dealing with international conflict. And yet the NCC could not bring itself to accept the Security Council's judgment that January 15, 1991—a date nearly half a year after the Iraqi invasion of Kuwait—constituted a reasonable deadline for the unconditional withdrawal of Saddam Hussein's army of occupation, even after Saddam Hussein had crudely rebuffed U.N. Secretary General Javier Perez de Cuellar in his final attempt to get the Iraqis to abide by the resolutions of the Security Council. Since the NCC is not formally a pacifist organization, one can only conclude that the Council's rejection of the U.N. position on the Gulf crisis had a good deal to do with the fact of American leadership both in the Security Council and in the multilateral military force that would enforce the Security Council's resolutions.

Abdicating Responsibilities

The NCC's pusillanimity in the face of Saddam Hussein, and its quick reach for "moral equivalence" between the United States and Iraq, were not, of course, unexpected. Indeed, one of the great sadnesses in American religion today is the widespread expectation that the National Council of Churches will, on any given issue involving the United States and the world, further mortgage its already tattered claim to be any sort of moral mentor to the American body politic: not simply by what it says, but by the singular failure of its leadership to learn anything from the NCC's errors of moral and political judgment over the past generation.

That case was put, interestingly enough, by a group of Czechoslovakian Christian activists who asked American Protestants to disregard the NCC's Gulf pronouncements. Said the Czechs to the Americans, "Your church representatives have underestimated the criminal nature of the Marxist regimes. Now they underestimate the criminal nature of the regime of Saddam Hussein. . . . We do not trust your church representatives who in the name of peace hamper the Gulf-area initiative of your president."[12] It was a damning indictment, but like so many other such indictments in recent years, it had no discernible effect on the leadership of the NCC.

There was one new player in the NCC's cast of political characters on the Gulf crisis, though: Jim Wallis, the editor of *Sojourners* magazine, and a twenty-year veteran of radical politics who now couches his judgments in terms of "prophetic" Christianity. Just before the NCC-coordinated "Church Leaders' Peace Pilgrimage to the Middle East" (in which he participated), Wallis circulated a memorandum (dated December 13, 1990) with his analysis of the Gulf crisis. Parts of that memorandum appeared, verbatim, eight days later in the "message to the American people" issued by the "church leaders" after they had putatively consulted with religious and political leaders in the region: which not only casts further doubt on the open-mindedness with which the church leaders undertook their "peace pilgrimage," but also illustrates the important role that Wallis—who long ago transcended moral equivalence and is firmly lodged in the camp of those who blame America first, early, and often—now plays at the higher altitudes of the NCC. One would be hard put to call this a marriage made in heaven; but as to the couple's compatibility, there can be little doubt.

U.S. Catholic Bishops and the War

The formal response of the U.S. Catholic bishops to the Gulf crisis was of a higher caliber of moral reflection than could be found in the pronouncements of the National Council of Churches. Gulf politics had dominated debate at the bishops' annual meeting in November 1990, and out of that meeting had come two letters: one by Archbishop Roger Mahony (addressed to Secretary of State James Baker in Mahony's capacity as chairman of the bishops' committee on international policy), and a second from the National Conference of

Catholic Bishops' chairman Archbishop Daniel Pilarczyk (addressed to President Bush).

Between these letters lay two vigorous debates, one in a closed executive session, in which the left wing of the bishops' conference, led by veteran Pax Christi activists such as Detroit auxiliary bishop Thomas Gumbleton, had pressed for an outright proscription on the use of U.S. military force in the Gulf. The body of bishops was not prepared to go so far as Gumbleton wished, and indeed the Mahony and Pilarczyk letters were explicitly couched in the just war language and style of moral reasoning that Pax Christi effectively rejects. But the net result was to yield an NCCB position that was widely, and not altogether inaccurately, reported by the prestige press as a Catholic rejection of Bush administration Gulf policy.

The bishops' position, as articulated in the Mahony and Pilarczyk letters and in subsequent testimony before the Senate Foreign Relations Committee by Archbishop John Roach (Mahony's successor as chairman of the committee on international policy),[13] laid great stress on the efficacy of economic sanctions as a means to bring about Saddam Hussein's unconditional withdrawal from Kuwait—a position shared, of course, by a number of prominent political and military analysts, including former national security advisor Zbigniew Brzezinski and former joint chiefs chairman Admiral William Crowe. But there were two other dimensions to the sanctions issue, neither of which received sufficient attention in the bishops' letters and testimony.

Misunderstanding Just War Criteria

On the empirical side of the affair, there was the devastating report issued by House Armed Services Committee chairman Les Aspin, which argued at great length and with considerable force that sanctions would never work—if by "work" one meant both the unconditional withdrawal of Iraq from Kuwait and the dismantling of Iraq's vast arsenal of offensive weaponry. More to the point, the bishops' letters and testimony never engaged the *moral* dilemma of a sanctions policy, which lay in the fact that economic sanctions would be felt first and hardest by those whom the just war tradition requires us to treat as noncombatants (i.e., the ordinary people of Iraq, whom President Bush had insisted were not our enemy), and only last by those whom we were most concerned to sway—the military-political leadership of the Saddam Hussein regime. There was, in other words, a just war "problem" with the sanctions policy, and it went unacknowledged in the bishops' letters and testimony.

The Mahony and Pilarczyk letters, and the Roach testimony, also put great stress on the just war criterion of "last resort," as indeed they should have. But the bishops seemed to treat "last resort" as virtually an arithmetic concept, which is not the way the world, or the just war tradition, works. One could always imagine "one more" non-military initiative that could be tried, in a sequence that by definition is infinite in duration.

No, what the tradition means by "last resort" is that all reasonable efforts at a non-military solution have been tried and have failed. In the face of Iraqi foreign minister Tariq Aziz's behavior at his Geneva meeting with U.S. Secretary of State James Baker on January 9, 1991, and Saddam Hussein's rebuff of the Perez de Cuellar and French initiatives in the last hours before the U.N. deadline of January 15, it is difficult to argue with President Bush's judgment that all reasonable non-military remedies had been exhausted.

Both the Mahony and Pilarczyk letters, and the Roach testimony, put great stress on an alleged shift in U.S. policy in early November 1990, when U.S. forces were enhanced so as to provide what the bishops persistently described as an "offensive" U.S. military capability in the Gulf. This, the bishops seemed to suggest, changed the moral calculus in some important way. And yet it is difficult to see how, unless one falls into the moral and political trap of assuming that "peace" prevailed in the Gulf between August 2, 1990, and January 17, 1991, the difference between "peace" and "war" being U.S. military engagement with Saddam's forces.

But this was palpably not the case, as President Bush said, simply and with great effect, in his address to the nation on the night of January 17. Military action to repel aggression, deter future aggression, and enforce international norms of conduct according to the authority of both the Security Council and the United States Congress does not constitute "offensive military action" in the sense that the United States was somehow initiating combat for aggressive ends. Saddam Hussein started the Gulf War on August 2, 1990. The remaining question was whether the war could be ended, on terms that met the criteria of the just war tradition as a moral calculus of statecraft and that satisfied Catholic understandings of a just peace, through other-than-military means. It would have been helpful if the bishops had acknowledged this.

More of the Same Vacuity

The Catholic debate over Gulf policy, beyond the confines of the NCCB and the United States Catholic Conference, was depressingly reminiscent of the vacuities that marked the NCC's engagement with the issue. Pax Christi indulged in a classic bit of moral equivalence in a lengthy ad it ran in the *National Catholic Reporter*, which argued that Bush administration Gulf policy "polarizes the region by demanding loyalty to one side or the other, rather than requiring that the world listen to both." (One wonders what Pax Christi thought it would hear from Saddam Hussein.) Nor did Pax Christi resist the temptation to use the Gulf crisis to plug other items on its ideological agenda: "This crisis is a painful reminder of our complicity in patterns of consumption to support a lifestyle that is fundamentally unjust and excessively wasteful. By our actions, we have shown that we are ready to kill and we are ready to die, but we are unwilling to curb our ecologically disastrous consumption habits."[14]

The inadequate, albeit serious, statements of Archbishops Mahony, Pilarczyk, and Roach were subsequently vulgarized by individual bishops in the days immediately preceding the engagement of U.S. forces with Saddam Hussein's military machine, as may be seen in comments made by auxiliary bishop William Curlin of Washington, D.C., and Bishop Walter Sullivan of Richmond (the incoming president of Pax Christi). Bishop Curlin, in a homily delivered at the National Shrine of the Immaculate Conception on January 13, made the remarkable historical judgment that "there are no winners when wars are ended—there are only losers" and, noting America's continued problems with homelessness, abortion, alcoholism, drug addiction, and racial injustice, asked, "Who are we to say we have the answers for justice in our world?" (According to the Curlin Rules, the United States should not have acted to resist fascist aggression in the 1940s, because there would only be losers in such a fray, because Jim Crow laws were on the books in dozens of states, and because the armed forces were officially segregated.)[15]

Bishop Sullivan, as is his wont from time to time, took matters considerably further, suggesting that Catholics in the military consider disobeying orders to participate in this war "which the Catholic Church considers unjustified and immoral."[16] That judgment had not, of course, been made, in those precise terms—unless one is to consider as the teaching of "the Catholic Church" the construal of NCCB documents by the Bishop of Richmond.

Another Voice Is Heard

Of far more concern for the future of the Catholic debate (in America and elsewhere) was the position taken by the

Rome-based Jesuit periodical *La Civiltà Cattolica*, whose editorials are frequently vetted by the Vatican secretariat of state and are thus often assumed to have a quasi-official status. The November 17, 1990, issue of the journal made a number of highly contingent judgments about modern warfare—that its "nature" had changed fundamentally; that noncombatant immunity was a thing of the past; that any war inevitably involved "not only two or more nations but directly or indirectly the planet"—and concluded that "war today, except in the case of defending oneself from a grave aggression underway, is morally unacceptable, whatever the reasons given for its justification."[17]

Reports as to the status of this editorial in terms of its reflecting official Vatican policy have varied, some denying that it in fact carried the *imprimatur* of the secretariat of state. Be that as it may, the editorial clearly identifies two critical points of friction between some currents in contemporary Catholic thought and the evolving just war teaching of the Holy See. The first of these friction points has to do with the Catholic understanding of "just cause." Papal teaching, since World War II, has drawn the boundaries of "just cause" ever more narrowly, doubtless in part because of the threat of nuclear war in a world dominated by the Cold War.

Yet in the post–Cold War world, inhabited as it is by such as Saddam Hussein (whose plunder of Kuwait for seven months, and whose military conduct after January 17, 1991, demonstrated beyond doubt his utter disdain for civilized norms of international behavior), cannot one make the case, and without opening the floodgates to Hobbes's war of all-against-all, for a revivification of the notion of "punishment for evil" as one of the legitimate component parts of a "just cause"? Surely the question is worth pursuing rather than dismissing out of hand.

Then there is the question of modern weapons technology and the just war tradition. The *Civiltà Cattolica* editorial, reflecting a widespread opinion in Catholic moral-theological circles, assumes that modern weaponry is inherently disproportionate and indiscriminate. And yet the extraordinary advances in precision-targeting graphically illustrated by the performance of the Tomahawk cruise missile and U.S. "smart bombs" during the air campaign against Iraq (and particularly against Baghdad) suggest that the opposite may be closer to the truth: modern weapons technology makes "proportionate" and "discriminate" use of armed force far more likely than it was when Father John Ford, S.J., wrote his seminal 1944 essay, "On the Morality of Obliteration Bombing."[18] At the very least, some reconsideration of the assumptions about modern weaponry that informed the *Civiltà Cattolica* editorial seem in order.

The Triumph of Functional Pacifism

Those who thought that anti–anti-communism was the driving ideological force behind the politics of the religious Left (which has long included much of the mainline/oldline leadership, and which has made a deep impact on the foreign policy views of more of the Catholic episcopate than one might think) were mistaken. The deepest taproot of the politics of the religious Left is its profound skepticism about the American experiment. A racist, imperialist, militarist, and, latterly, sexist America cannot act for good ends in the world. That is thc orthodoxy in thc NCC and in a depressingly large part of the Catholic episcopate. And the orthopraxis follows with inexorable logic: resistance to American power—not resistance to Saddam Hussein's aggression—is the index by which one measures one's commitment to "peace."

Theological vs. Political Pacifism

An American Christian leadership that had concluded, in conscience, that the Gospel demanded a pacifist position would be an American Christian leadership worthy of respect. It would be a religious leadership with which one could engage in honest conversation about the relationship between religiously derived moral norms and the exigencies of public life. But a religious leadership whose views of international politics derive from forms of Christian sentimentality that effectively deny the classic Christian notion of the brokenness of creation, a religious leadership that is palpably alienated from even a critical affection for the American experiment and what it means for the world—that is a religious leadership that will become, as it in many respects has already become, utterly marginal to the public moral argument about the right-ordering of our society, and the definition of its role in the world.

And yet the themes of disaffection from the American experiment that grounded so much of the mainline/oldline and NCC commentary on the Gulf crisis continued in the war's aftermath. The *Christian Century*, flagship opinion journal of the liberal Protestant establishment, opined in an April 17, 1991, editorial that the lesson of the war was that "there were gods on our side, gods that are worshipped by the American people: the twin gods of financial power and military security."[19]

Nor did the immediate post-war commentary in certain Catholic circles do much to give one confidence that reflection on the Gulf crisis would become the occasion for a more thoughtful American Catholic appropriation of the just war tradition. Richard D. Parry, for example, writing in the national Jesuit periodical *America*, suggested that the just war tradition was the result of a fundamental corruption that occurred when the "peace tradition of Christianity" was abandoned at the time of Constantine (a historically dubious proposition at best, yet one that has increasing resonance in many influential Catholic circles), and argued that "the most dismaying outcome of the [Gulf crisis] discussion within the

Church is how inconclusive it was"—as if the just war tradition were a kind of intellectual cookie-cutter out of which could be produced ready-made answers to extraordinarily complex issues at the intersection of morality and strategy.[20]

In light of all this, and fully conceding that there is ample room (and reason) to criticize the post-war actions of the Bush administration in respect to the disposition of Iraq and the plight of the Iraqi Shi'ites and Kurds, the conclusion that almost certainly has to be drawn from the mainline/oldline and Catholic address to the Gulf crisis must be that the leadership of these two critical sectors of American Christianity is now functionally pacifist in its politics. This is not, it must be emphasized, a pacifism of moral principle. Rather it is a functional pacifism rooted, for many oldline Protestant leaders in particular, in a profound alienation from the American experiment and in a deep conviction that American power cannot serve good ends in the world.

Indeed, the actions taken by the National Council of Churches, and by the more radical wing of the Catholic leadership, were grounded, not in a concern that American military action would fail, but in a deep fear that it would succeed. And were it to succeed, these men and women instinctively understood, that would be the end of "Vietnam," the prism through which their politics had been focused for a generation and the paradigm by which they had persistently read (which is to say, misread) the international politics of the 1970s and 1980s.

Justice Abandoned

For here, after all, was a possible use of American military force that ought to have drawn the support of mainline/oldline and Catholic leaders, *and precisely in terms of their own professed principles and regional concerns*. A brutal dictator, armed to the teeth with offensive military capabilities and busily developing weapons of mass destruction (including those nuclear weapons that had so exercised religious leaders in the early 1980s) invades, occupies, and dismantles a neighboring country. The invaded country is an Arab country, with a substantial number of Palestinian workers. The leading Arab financial power (Saudi Arabia) and the leading Arab military power (Egypt) support the United States in its resistance to Iraqi aggression. The president locates U.S. policy in terms of supporting a "new world order" in which the rule of law replaces the law of the jungle. The United Nations, in an unprecedented collective security action, moves against the aggressor. The Soviet Union joins with the United States in garnering the votes on the Security Council. A program of economic sanctions is undertaken. Israel stays on the sidelines. The world decides, through the Security Council, that enough time has expired: Saddam has been in Kuwait for five-and-a-half months, on any day of which he could have brought the Gulf crisis to a non-military resolution by the simple expedient of withdrawing his army of occupation. The Security Council and the Congress authorize the use of U.S. armed forces. Our Arab allies join us in the campaign.

If, under *these* circumstances, the leaders of oldline Protestantism and American Catholicism cannot bring themselves to say, yes, here is a situation in which the use of proportionate and discriminate armed force is morally justifiable, then it is hard to imagine what use of U.S. military power these religious leaders would ever sanction. They have, to repeat, become functional pacifists.

And in doing so, they have abandoned one of their most precious slogans, that of "peace and justice." There was virtually no attempt to maintain *this* form of "linkage" in the church debate on the Gulf. "Justice" was abandoned, as the NCC had long ago (in the days of the Cold War) abandoned "freedom" as a political component of peace. What has been left is a debased concept of "peace" that has long been regarded as morally suspect by both the just war and pacifist traditions: "peace" as the mere absence of conflict. Yet one can only conclude that, for much of the country's religious leadership, the debasement has gone even further: "peace" is the absence of armed American engagement with international conflict. How else can one understand the bizarre claims that "peace" reigned in the Gulf until January 17, 1991, and that the United States initiated the "war" that ensued, then and only then?

THE FUTURE OF THE DEBATE

America could have used a religiously grounded peace movement worthy of the name during the Gulf crisis—which was precisely not what mainline/oldline Protestantism and Catholic activists offered the country. Why would such a peace movement have been helpful? Because it would have clarified the debate over the ends and means of American power in the post–Cold War world. And because the alternative to a peace movement that embodies and teaches the wisdom of centuries of Christian social-ethical reflection is (as was so clearly demonstrated during the Gulf crisis) an anti-American power (military or otherwise) movement that will continue to devalue the currency of public moral argument in a manner that should be familiar to anyone over the age of thirty-five.

What would a religiously grounded peace movement worthy of the name have said during the Gulf crisis, and beginning on August 2, 1990?

It would have made unambiguously clear, from the outset, its rejection of Iraqi aggression. It would have told Saddam Hussein that he must not count on playing the "Vietnam card" in American domestic politics.

It would have condemned the Iraqi dictator's relentless buildup of weapons of mass destruction and demanded their dismantling under credible forms of international inspection.

It would have avoided Saddam Hussein's strategic trap: the establishment of a fictitious moral equivalence between the Iraqi invasion, occupation, plunder, and attempted annexation of Kuwait, on the one hand, and Israeli policy (which is surely not beyond criticism) in the occupied territories.

It would have taken its own professed concerns about international law seriously, rather than mourning that the United Nations had become an instrument of American imperial purpose.

It would have refused to indulge in various forms of corporation-bashing, and it would have disciplined itself to reject such infantile slogans as "We won't fight for Texaco." It would have linked legitimate concerns about America's dependence on foreign oil to an acknowledgment that the countries that would be hit hardest by Saddam Hussein's control over this basic commodity would be the poorest countries of the Third World and the emerging democracies of Central and Eastern Europe.

It would have avoided any apologies for the embrace of Saddam Hussein by the PLO and its chairman, Yasir Arafat.

It would have understood, with Bernard Lewis, that "the only true solution [for the Arabs] . . . is to free themselves from the variegated tyrannies that oppress and degrade them, and to create new regimes, more respectful of human and political rights, their own and other people's."[21]

It would have brought its concern for nonviolence to bear on the central historic tragedy of the post–World War II Arab world: that its defining characteristic is political violence, within Arab countries and between Arab countries. It would have said, again with Lewis, that the development of a more humane political culture in the Arab Middle East is "not beyond the creative powers of a great and gifted people whose forebears wrote one of the most brilliant chapters in the history of civilization."[22] It would, in other words, have refused to engage in that liberal racism that treats Arabs as so many fractious children who really don't know any better, and thus have to be appeased.

It would not even have hinted that the moral argument on U.S. Gulf policy was one between the morally concerned and the morally obtuse. Moreover, it would have celebrated the great public moral argument that did take place between August 1990 and January 1991 as a complex democratic deliberation on the real-world application of the central political virtue of prudence.

A Distorted View of America

Finally, it would have gotten itself straightened out on the subject of America. Has there ever been so reluctant a superpower as the United States? Has there ever been a great power, at the pinnacle of world politics and economics, that put itself through such a rigorous self-examination before it committed its citizens to battle? U.S. foreign policy is neither omniscient nor omnicompetent, and it is surely less than wholly satisfactory from a moral perspective. The errors of U.S. policy toward Iraq in the 1980s were manifold, and there is reason to worry that similar misunderstandings of the politics of the Middle East have played too large a role in shaping post-war U.S. policy in that volatile region.

But to suggest, as some prominent figures in the religious agitations against U.S. military engagement with Saddam Hussein did, that America was more of a threat to peace than the Iraqi dictator is a position so extravagantly wrongheaded that it can only derive, not from a careful and prudent moral calculus of the ends and means of power, but from a deep-set alienation that constitutes the temporal and ideological link between much of the American religious leadership and "Vietnam."

Winning the Peace

Had such a religiously grounded peace movement emerged during the Gulf crisis, it would have been in a strong position to help shape the public moral argument over how America might help win the peace, having won the war.

The just war tradition, which is the normative Western moral tradition for thinking about issues at the intersection of religiously grounded moral norms and international public life, is more than a moral calculus for determining when the resort to armed force is morally justified and how that armed force is to be used in a justified war. For in addition to the classic *ius ad bellum* and *ius in bello*, the just war tradition contains a *ius ad pacem*—a theory of statecraft in which is embedded an important concept of peace.

The theory of statecraft implicit in the just war tradition requires that the proportionate and discriminate use of armed force be ordered to the pursuit of peace in all its component parts: freedom, justice, security, and order. The peace envisioned by the tradition is not the utopian vision of a world without conflict, but the peace of a world in which law and politics—rightly ordered legal and political institutions—are the normal means of prosecuting and resolving conflict. Any "new world order," in other words, need not be tethered to a Wilsonian naïveté about the nature of politics among nations. A "new world order" can and should be built on the far sturdier foundations of Augustinian realism—amplified by a little of the optimism about human possibilities that characterized the political thought of Thomas Aquinas.

What might a religious peace movement grounded in these ancient truths of the Christian tradition have said about the pursuit of peace in the post-war Middle East? It would not have said any one thing, for the tradition is too subtle, and the Middle East too complex, for any responsible person to argue that there is one "Christian position" on the pursuit of peace with freedom and justice in the Levant. On the other hand, how much better off would the public discourse have been, had the leadership of American Christianity, in active conversation with Jewish and Muslim interlocutors, pressed the following package of peace initiatives into the debate?

1. Peace-for-Peace

The Gulf War—the fact that it happened, and the dynamics of the coalition politics by which it was fought—should have put to rest the notion (depressingly ubiquitous in the American mainline and Roman Catholic leadership) that the "Palestinian question" is the cause of all the other woes of the Middle East. That was never the case. The two central problems that must be addressed, if there is to be even a minimum of order in the Middle East, are the continuing Arab war against Israel and the instability of Arab political regimes.

With the honorable exception of Egypt, virtually the entire Arab world has been in a formal state of war with Israel since 1948—forty-three years. The American religious community could have insisted that, until that brute fact is changed, there is no path to peace open in the region. The state of war against Israel must end.

When the Gulf war ended on February 27, 1991, the United States was in a position of extraordinary leverage throughout the Middle East, and between the Middle East and those parts of the world with economic, political, and religious interests in the region. Why could not the American religious community have urged on the U.S. government that this was the moment to press our Arab coalition partners to take the lead in "peace-for-peace": to declare the forty-three-year-old war with Israel to be at an end, and to recognize (through an exchange of diplomatic missions and an end to the Arab economic boycott) the permanent reality of Israel in the Middle East, without foreclosing any future arguments about the final disposition of borders in the region.

The American religious community, and particularly its formal leadership, could have taken the lead in teaching that land-for-peace is a non-starter, and that peace-for-peace is where the path to peace begins. In doing so, it would have made an important break with the drift toward psychological concepts of peace that were too frequently characteristic of American Christian activism over the past generation, and it would have given new concreteness to the political concept of peace lodged within the just war tradition.

2. Economic Development

There was much talk during the Gulf crisis, in the religious press and among religious opinion elites, about the "unjust distribution of wealth" in the Middle East, by which it was usually meant that there is considerable poverty in an area awash in wealth from the sale of oil—an indisputable fact of life in the region. But the religious agitations against U.S. policy in the Gulf took the argument yet another step and suggested that this problem was, somehow, the fault of "the West" (and specifically of the oil-consumption habits of the American people), although the price of crude oil is set by OPEC and the distribution of monies generated thereby is, in the main, in the hands of Arabs.

One need not doubt that the sense of distributive justice is not entirely overdeveloped in some Arab ruling families. And perhaps, in the wake of the Gulf War, a sense of self-preservation will compensate for this lack of a sense of distributive justice, with the result being a more thoughtful use of the oil riches of the region.

Still, the religious community might have taken the lead in driving the debate beyond the sterilities of gas pricing debates by suggesting that the pursuit of peace in the Middle East, according to the understanding of "peace" embedded in the Christian tradition, might require something more than a more equitable distribution of existing oil wealth. Had they not been so beholden to the politics of redistribution, and had they been attentive to the realities of wealth creation, the nation's religious leadership could have urged the development of cooperative economic enterprises in which peoples now divided by tribe, race, or religion could work together to create new wealth and to better their own economic circumstances: on the admittedly crude, but empirically verifiable, rule-of-thumb which states that people engaged in making money together are less likely to be found cutting each other's throats at the first opportunity. Why, for example, could the religious leadership not have proposed the creation of a Jordan Valley Development Authority that would bring Israelis, Jordanians, Lebanese, and now-stateless Palestinians together in a common economic enterprise aimed at common problems: declining water resources; lack of electricity and other key elements of modern infrastructure; deforestation and soil erosion; inadequate irrigation?

A vaguely anti-bourgeois sensibility has been one ideological current in mainline/oldline Protestantism, and in some significant Catholic circles, for over a generation now. That animus has blocked the nation's religious leadership from understanding that the sooner the Middle East develops a broad middle class, the sooner it is likely to abandon its current style of political, religious, and ethnic mayhem. Economic development schemes aimed at creating that middle class, even through experiments in joint economic activity, would seem to be a concrete expression of the churches' oft-stated concern for "economic justice."

3. *Regional Security Issues*

Churches are not diplomatic or military agencies, although some church leaders seem to have no end of trouble remembering that. It is not the business of the Church, as the Church, to devise regional security schemes for the Middle East, or anywhere else, for that matter. But a religious leadership trying to think through the implications of the just war tradition's concept of peace for the Middle East might well have proposed, in broad terms, a number of regional security initiatives, including vigorous arms control efforts (aimed at preventing the introduction of more weapons of mass destruction into the region); the thinning out of conventional forces throughout the Middle East; the elimination of all weapons of mass destruction; the phased elimination of ballistic missiles from the Middle East; and far more restrictive Western policies on technology transfer, so as to lessen the likelihood that Western high-technology brought into the region for peaceful purposes will reignite a Levantine arms race, in either conventional or unconventional terms.

4. *Pre-Democratization*

The mainline/oldline commentary on international affairs in the past decade has been conspicuously silent on the democratic revolution and its implications for the prospects of peace with freedom, justice, security, and order. Nuclear-weapons phobias in the early 1980s misdirected religious attention from the source of the East-West conflict in Europe and from the importance, precisely for the cause of peace, of human rights initiatives aimed at building civil society as the foundation of democratic transitions in the communist world. In the Gulf conflict, the churches were, for the most part, just as inattentive to the democratic stirrings that were beginning to be heard from some quarters in the Arab world.

Democracy is no panacea for the tangled and ancient conflicts of the Middle East. But from the point of view of Christian social ethics, which has laid great stress in recent years on the protection of basic human rights, it is surely worthwhile for American Christian leaders to support efforts to help lay down the building blocks of democratic culture throughout the Arab Middle East: a freer press; consultative assemblies, as the staging grounds for genuine legislatures; legally protected opposition political parties; trade unions and business associations; and voluntary organizations, including human rights groups. One would also have liked to have heard more from American Christian leaders about the acute problems of religious freedom in the Arab Middle East, and one would have liked to have seen more attention paid to how inter-religious conversation between American Christians and American Muslims might help advance the cause of religious freedom throughout the world. Such attention would seem to be mandated by the dictates of Christian conscience; it might also have a salutary effect, over the long haul, on the prospects for a more decent and humane politics in the Middle East.

5. *The Palestinians*

Over the past decade, mainline/oldline Protestantism has adopted the Palestinian cause in a manner strikingly parallel to that in which liberal Protestantism's "social justice" curias adopted the Nicaraguan Sandinistas and the Salvadoran FMLN during the debates over U.S. policy in Central America in the late 1970s and early 1980s. Indeed, less than twenty-four hours after the ceasefire in the Gulf was announced, the National Council of Churches released a statement claiming that "the pursuit of peace [in the Middle East] must begin with the recognition of the legitimate rights of the Palestinian people to self-determination and a home of their own. . . ."[23]

And yet the sad truth of the matter is that the "Palestinian problem" got worse during the Gulf War, rather than better —a point that a serious, religiously grounded peace movement would have frankly confronted. The Israeli peace camp, some of whose leaders hold political views to the left of even the National Council of Churches, was shaken to its foundations by the sight of Palestinians cheering Scud missile attacks on civilian centers in Tel Aviv and Haifa, the same Palestinians who demanded gas masks while calling on Saddam Hussein to launch chemical warfare against Israel.

Such incomprehensibly self-defeating behavior is often dismissed, and by more than a few American religious leaders, as the result of "desperation." Yet no prominent leader of mainline/oldline Protestantism or the National Council of Churches has yet taken the Palestinians seriously enough to tell them candidly that the time for psychobabble has ended, and that today's claims of "desperation" are less than plausible in light of the fact that similar claims were made when Palestinian leaders embraced the Soviet Union during the Cold War, and when the Grand Mufti of Jerusalem embraced Hitler during World War II.

A religious peace movement worthy of the name would have been quietly grateful for the dramatic discrediting of Yasir Arafat and the PLO during the Gulf War, for it would have understood that Arafat's decline opened up the possibility that a new Palestinian leadership might emerge, through open and carefully monitored elections in the occupied territories. Should that happen, American religious institutions and leaders serious about the pursuit of peace with freedom and justice in the Middle East would publicly urge that new Palestinian leadership to engage in the kind of peace process envisioned above: a commitment to peace-for-peace, unambiguously recognizing the permanence of Israel in the region; participation in joint regional economic development projects; an end to Palestinian terrorism and a commitment to a disarmed Palestinian homeland; and democratization, including the creation and legal protection of multiple Palestinian political parties and a free Palestinian press.

Challenging Realpolitik

Having brought this kind of a package of peace initiatives to the public debate, a religious peace movement that took seriously the concept of worldly peace embedded in the just war tradition would have been in a stronger position to urge both Israel and the United States to a more imaginative and supple diplomacy in the Middle East: Israel, in terms of a creative rethinking of its occupation policies in the territories and its long-term security requirements; the United States, in terms of the perennial tendency of American policymakers to defer unduly to the narrow concerns of certain favored Arab states and their ruling families as the baseline for U.S. policy in the Arab Middle East.

It seems clear, in the aftermath of the Gulf War, that the American-led coalition that fought the war to a militarily successful conclusion had a far more sophisticated and comprehensive plan for winning the war than it did for winning the peace in the post-war Gulf and throughout the Middle East. Perhaps such a comprehensive settlement is simply impossible at this moment in history. But a religious leadership that had more accurately read the sources of conflict in the region, and that had not mortgaged itself to the politically driven "prophetic stance" of such as Jim Wallis, might have been able to set down some needed markers for the post-war debate over the possibilities of peace in the Middle East. At the very least, it would have been better positioned to challenge the appeals to a new realpolitik—understood in some quarters to be an alternative to "Wilsonian moralism," but in truth simply a debased form of moral reasoning—that were heard from both left and right in the post-war debate over U.S. and coalition responsibilities for the Kurds and Shi'ites who had challenged the Saddam Hussein regime.

Christianity and Islam

The Gulf crisis was also the first occasion to test (and in the context of a historic crisis with grave consequences for the parties involved) the churches' recent interest in an expanded dialogue with the many worlds of Islam. One would be hard put to argue, in the wake of the crisis, that the test was passed *cum laude*.

Before, during, and after the Gulf War, religious publications across the Christian spectrum published a large amount of foolishness about Islam, its basic tenets, its relationship to what in the West is understood as "politics," and its self-understanding vis-à-vis Judaism and Christianity: thus illustrating, in the most graphic terms, that the basic Western problem in the face of the challenge of Islam in the post–Cold War world is ignorance (an ignorance that often affects the teaching elites of American Christianity, alas). Discussions of Islam and its relationship to the Gulf crisis were also distorted by the dubious assumptions about the politics of the Arab Middle East noted above.

A Tradition Misread

A striking example of the intellectual problems and historical confusions that often bedevil Christian attempts to reach out to the Islamic world—which is, in part, an honorable effort to open the path of dialogue with a great cultural tradition; in part, an exercise in *Tercermundismo* (the Arabs of the Middle East, and especially the Palestinians, having replaced the campesinos of Latin America as the favored "wretched of the earth"); and in part, yet another example of the seemingly irresistible temptation to blame the West first—could be found in a statement by an American Jesuit, Father Thomas Michel, S.J. Father Michel's remarks, delivered in Rome on February 15, 1991, are of particular interest for two reasons: first, because he is the secretary of the Vatican's Commission for Religious Relations with the Muslims; and second, because the speech was subsequently reprinted in *La Civiltà Cattolica* (whose semi-official relationship with the Vatican Secretariat of State has been noted above) and in *Origins*, the documentary service of the USCC's Catholic News Service—thus insuring Father Michel a large and influential American Christian audience.

One premise of Father Michel's lecture was that Islam has been poorly reported in the Western press, and that these media caricatures have created a warped view of Islamic convictions and practice that in turn distorts Western policies toward the Arab Middle East. The first half of the premise can be readily conceded: an American prestige press that cannot differentiate among the divergent worlds of American evangelicals and fundamentalists, and that practices ideological spin control in its coverage of the Catholic Church in the United States, is not, *prima facie*, likely to do much better by Islam.[24]

Father Michel was also surely right to remind us that there are many forms of "Islamic fundamentalism," and that lumping together under that rubric "such radically different people and movements as Ayatollah Khomeini, King Fahd of Saudi Arabia, Moammar Gadhafi, the Muslim Brotherhood, the pacifist Tabligh movement, Saddam Hussein, and the Jama'at-i-Islami movement of the Indian subcontinent" is quite wrongheaded.[25]

Further, Father Michel's lecture usefully clarified the multiple meanings of *jihad* in Islam, and conceded that, in its third sense of the struggle "to oppose injustice and oppression, when necessary, by force," the concept of *jihad* can be "manipulated by a [political] leader who can call a religious *jihad* for motives that in fact stem from ambition, power, vendetta, or riches."[26]

These important and helpful points having been made, however, the Michel lecture then became the occasion for a highly tendentious reading of the history of the Arab Middle East, including dubious assertions about the continuing force and importance of pan-Arabism; a defense of the most implausible of Third World apologies for the behavior of Saddam Hussein; an attack on continuing Western "imperialism"; and an extraordinary statement of theological equivalence between Islam and Christianity:

• "All those who know Iraqis," wrote Father Michel, "know that they have always considered Kuwait an integral part of their country. This explains the widespread support that Saddam's decision [to invade] found among his own people."[27]

Widespread support? In a totalitarian state run by perhaps the world's most brutal internal security system? In a state which Father Michel concedes consists of three historically distinct provinces, two of which were instantaneously in revolt two weeks after Father Michel spoke of Saddam Hussein's "widespread support"?

• Moreover, Father Michel continued, "since the Arabs consider themselves a single people artificially divided into various states, their nationalistic sentiments are always oriented more toward the unity of the Arab people . . ."[28]—a judgment that rather defies charitable description, given the coalition politics of the Gulf War, much less the history of intra-Arab violence in the post–World War II period.

• Father Michel then took a therapeutic turn, analyzing international politics through the prism of personalist psychology, a familiar (if terribly misleading) tactic in some religious circles confronted with the intractability of certain conflicts in the world: ". . . There is general indignation [among Arabs] toward Western peoples, the feeling of being manipulated, exploited, and mistreated by the Europeans and, after World War II, by the Americans, to America's advantage. . . . This indignation is not only felt by the masses, but also by intellectuals, religious, the military, and politicians. . . . When a leader emerges like Gamal Abdel Nasser in the 1950s and today Saddam Hussein, who resists the pressures of Western powers and challenges their ultimatums, he appears a hero in the eyes of many."[29]

But does Father Michel mention the enormous damage Nasser and Saddam Hussein did to their own societies, and to the region? No. Does Father Michel mention that the extraordinary wealth of the Arab Middle East is the result of the transfer of immense amounts of Western dollars, Deutschmarks, pounds, francs, and, latterly, yen into Arab hands? No. Does Father Michel suggest that the perennial assumption of one's status as victim can become a socio-cultural neurosis with debilitating (and often violent) political ramifications? No.

• Father Michel also reports that, in the Arab world, "there is a frequently expressed feeling [again, the word "feeling"] that 'the West wishes to destroy Islam.' "[30]

But does Father Michel even hint that such a "feeling" is best described, to adopt his psychological categories, as paranoid? No.

• Finally, there is the matter of Christianity and Islam. The "teaching on the Islamic ideals," writes Father Michel, "shows they are not very different from those of Christians: to believe in a God who has created all things, has a moral will according to which all will be judged, who rewards the good and punishes evildoers, leaves people free to choose and immediately forgives anyone who repents, etc."[31]

Glossing Over Difficulties

But surely these points of moral tangency, which could become the basis for a more serious Christian-Islamic dialogue over time, have to be understood in a more sophisticated theological context that faces, without denial or hysteria, the reality of Islamic supersessionism, i.e., Islam's conviction that the revelation to Mohammed has superseded the revelations to Abraham and Jesus. Father Michel notes with satisfaction that the Second Vatican Council's Declaration on the Relationship of the Church to Non-Christian Religions, *Nostra Aetate*, calls Christians to look upon Muslims "with esteem."[32] Unhappily, as Father Michel does not note, there is no Muslim *Nostra Aetate* (although there are surely individual Muslims whose practice of religious tolerance is quite admirable).

Nor did Father Michel, lecturing in February 1991, have anything of consequence to say about the rape and pillage of Kuwait; or about the difficulties (acknowledged by senior Vatican officials) in engaging Muslim interlocutors in a serious interfaith dialogue;[33] or about the state of religious liberty in the Arab Middle East (and this despite the pope's sharp words on the subject). Father Michel may think that, in his lecture, he was observing Luther's injunction in the *Small Catechism*, that Christians should put the best possible construction on everything. Yet some ways of acting on this honorable instinct so distort reality that they make serious conversation, and the exploration of real differences within the bond of civility, even more difficult.

Perhaps most distressingly, Father Michel made no mention of those scholars (and some activists) in the Islamic world who are trying to confront the historic political failures of Arab regimes, who are trying to effect what in the West would be called a "development of doctrine" by adumbrating a Qur'anically-based Islamic theory of religious liberty, and who are calling Arab nations to move down the path to democracy and to a more equitable distribution of oil wealth. Instead of highlighting these heartening developments—which in many cases emerge precisely from serious Islamic religious and moral concerns—Father Michel offered his audience the standard package of Arab political grievances as if these complaints, many of which rest on the shakiest of historical foundations, have a kind of privileged moral status in the debate.

A More Realistic Dialogue

A Christian-Islamic dialogue is, to state the obvious, badly needed. But not any "dialogue" will do. What Václav Havel called "living in the truth" in reference to the democratic transitions in Central and Eastern Europe has applications in the worlds of interfaith dialogue, too. And "living in the truth" in the context of the Christian-Islamic dialogue means facing two realities that, it should be frankly admitted, are in tension with each other.

The first reality that has to be faced is that modern Islamic societies display a pronounced tendency toward monism: they link family/tribe, state, and religion into a thick unity that is, *ex definitione*, antipluralistic, and quite probably incapable of sustaining a genuine democracy. Moreover, since the cultural (and religious) affirmation of legitimate pluralism as a positive social good seems to be a characteristic of the evolution of societies committed to the nonviolent resolution of conflict within and among nations, Islamic tendencies toward religio-socio-political monism have profound implications for the pursuit of peace in the Middle East.

On the other hand, there is the historic experience of medieval Islam, which provides ample testimony to the fact that Islam once provided religious legitimation for societies that practiced considerable tolerance. There are also those "dissidents" in the contemporary Islamic world noted just above, who are working (often at great personal risk) to develop an Islamic approach to the organization of modern society that makes the adhesion of Islamic states to the Universal Declaration of Human Rights far more of a reality than it is today. These dissidents are, to be sure, a minority in their countries, and in the wider context of the "house of Islam." But that fact simply reinforces the importance of Western religious leaders' offering support to those whose work holds out the prospect of a Christian-Islamic dialogue that involves more than shadow-boxing, with episodes of Christian self-flagellation between rounds.

Father Michel's intentions were, I am sure, honorable and humane. I have no doubt of his commitment to bridging the chasms of misunderstanding and hostility that now divide many parts of the Christian and Islamic worlds. But his lecture deserves critical attention and challenge precisely because it embodies, in compact form, so many of the assumptions and judgments that shaped (and, in my judgment, mis-shaped) mainline/oldline and Catholic commentary on the interface between Christianity and Islam during the Gulf crisis. That interface could well be of world-historical consequence in the twenty-first century—all the more reason to try to build the Christian-Islamic dialogue on firmer theological, historical, and political foundations than were evident in the commentary of too many Christian Islamicists during the Gulf war.[34]

Needed: A Theology of Peace

The key word in the previous sentence is, of course, "theological." Alienation from the American experiment shaped the *politics* of the religious Left during the war, as I argued above. But the root problem of the churches' engagement with the public moral argument that preceded U.S. military action in the Gulf, and that also bedeviled some church leaders' discussion of the future of Christian-Islamic relationships (particularly in the context of the politics of the Middle East), should not be located at the level of historical or political analysis, but in terms of doctrine. Mainline/oldline Protestantism and a considerable part of the Catholic leadership, having abandoned Christian Realism of the sort taught by Reinhold Niebuhr, Paul Ramsey, and John Courtney Murray, have substituted in its place psychologized and quasi-utopian understandings of international public life, which suggest the possibility of a world without conflict. What has been lost in this doctrinal shuffle is the classic Christian tradition's understanding of "peace" as *tranquillitas ordinis*: rightly ordered and dynamic political community, in and among nations, in which legal and political institutions provide effective means for resolving the inevitable conflicts that will define public life until the End Time.

While certain minority currents in the long, complex history of Christian social thought have argued for the possibility of man's building the promised Kingdom of peace and righteousness here on earth, the mainstream Christian tradition, even in its more optimistic reading of human possibilities (as in the Thomistic, Anabaptist, and Wesleyan traditions), has been resolutely anti-utopian, which is to say, Augustinian. The collapse of this Augustinian realism about human propensities for evil, cruelty, and injustice is one root of liberal Protestantism's and radical Catholicism's extreme skepticism about the just war tradition, whose origins are, of course, to be found in Augustine himself. And to jettison the just war tradition is to jettison the worldly concept of peace that, as has been argued so frequently in this essay, is embedded in it. But peace, according to Christian self-understandings, must still be pursued: which means, to come full circle, substituting for various utopianisms the peace of *tranquillitas ordinis*, the worldly peace of politics and law.

Biblical Peace and Worldly Peace

The path to a reformed American Christian address to the problems of war and peace in the post–Cold War world will run through a far more sophisticated theology of peace than is presently informing Christian activism on these issues. Such a theology would have several defining characteristics.

It would understand the biblical peace of *shalom*—the peace of the Kingdom of God established in its fullness, the peace in which swords are beaten into plowshares, the lions rest with the lambs, and the nations stream to the mountaintop of the Lord (Isaiah 2.2–4)—as an eschatological horizon toward which humanity is called, and against which the brokenness of the present world can be measured.

But it would also understand that the peace of *shalom* in its fullness is a matter of God's work, not man's, and it would thus eschew utopian notions of the mundane achievement of the peace of *shalom* through human agency—especially human political agency. *Shalom*-as-eschatological-horizon is thus an essential complement to the quotidian task of building the peace of *tranquillitas ordinis*—the peace of dynamic and rightly ordered political community, within and among nations—in this world, this side of the coming of the Kingdom. *Shalom* reminds us of the limits of the political, and thus clarifies just what is possible—and thus obligatory—for political life.

A reformed theology of peace within which *shalom* and *tranquillitas ordinis* stand in creative tension would reposition the just war tradition precisely as a moral calculus oriented toward the pursuit of peace with freedom, order, security, and justice. It would take as one of its primary tasks the development of the concept of statecraft implied by the just war tradition. And in doing so it would help establish, in the wider public debate over war and peace, that there is no escape from the rigors of moral reasoning in facing questions of America's role in world affairs. It would link concepts of national interest to concepts of national purpose and national responsibility. And thus it would challenge both Wilsonian moralism and those forms of realpolitik which seem to suggest that a sufficiently tough-minded construal of "the national interest" absolves one from further reflection on the "ought" questions in the foreign policy debate.

Reclaiming an Understanding of Justice

A reformed theology of peace would resist the temptation —still widespread in religious circles influenced by the theologies of liberation—to pose the achievement of "justice" as the absolute precondition to peace. The reformed theology of peace envisioned here would have a far more subtle and complex understanding of the relationship between these two moral ends of politics. It would reclaim the triadic conception of justice—as commutative, distributive, and legal—that once characterized Christian thought on these matters. And it would develop the notion that legal justice—questions of the constitutional and legal right-ordering of societies and polities—is fundamental to the pursuit of peace as *tranquillitas ordinis*.

A reformed theology of peace would thus reflect far more seriously on the experience of the Revolution of 1989 in Central and Eastern Europe—a revolution built primarily on demands for the protection of basic human rights and on demands for democratic governance, as the preconditions to the pursuit of more equitable economic arrangements. It would also understand that in a world in which there will always be conflicts over what is "just" in given situations, a key moral issue for those concerned about the pursuit of peace is the availability of nonviolent legal and political instruments for adjudicating those conflicting claims without mass violence.

The Lay Vocation in the World

A reformed theology of peace would also challenge the clericalism that was one of the notable characteristics of the churches' address to the Gulf crisis. It would understand that holy orders, however construed in the various Christian ecclesial communities, confer no special charism of worldly wisdom. It would take far more seriously the teaching of the Second Vatican Council that "on the national and international planes the field of the apostolate is vast; and *it is there that the laity more than others are the channels of Christian wisdom*."[35] In making the Council's teaching real in the life of the ecumenical Church, religious leaders, theologians, and Christian political theorists would engage a far wider array of fellow-Christian interlocutors in government, the military, and the relevant academic and policy disciplines than was the case with both the National Council of Churches and the United States Catholic Conference during the Gulf crisis. At the practical level, this will inevitably involve a reform of the bureaucratic processes by which denominations and ecumenical agencies gather information, form judgments, and make public statements on matters of war and peace.

A reformed theology of peace would take up another, and related, ecclesiological issue, namely, the appropriate roles of the Church in public moral argument about war and peace. The National Council of Churches' approach—reams of (usually tendentious and often partisan) policy analysis and prescription, preceded by a modicum of biblical/theological language—is clearly inadequate, and indeed ecclesiologically misconceived. The National Conference of Catholic Bishops made a serious effort in November 1990 to shape the public moral argument over the Gulf crisis according to the canons of the just war tradition, but Archbishop Roach's subsequent testimony before the Senate Foreign Relations Committee fell back into the familiar pattern, in which lengthy historical and policy analysis obscures and in some respects marginalizes the moral arguments being made.

The right "mix" of moral-framework setting and illustrative policy application is not easy to define in the abstract. But surely further conversation and debate on the balance here is in order. The churches are not perceived, by the wider political community (or indeed by many of their congregants), as wise moral counsellors or, as the Catholic bishops like to put it, as "pastors and teachers." They are perceived, and not without reason, as political, and indeed partisan, actors. The formal leadership of the churches has to face this fact, and it has to engage a serious debate about the ways in which religious leaders (and others, particularly the laity) embody the "public Church" in the public arena. The alternative to that conversation is a "public Church" that, in many respects, continues to drive itself to the margins of the debate, all the while consoling itself with the notion that it is being "prophetic."

Neither Victims Nor Executioners

Finally, a reformed theology of peace would insist that there is no escape from moral responsibility when the nation is faced with a challenge and a threat like that posed by Saddam Hussein's invasion and occupation of Kuwait. Those who, in the name of the peace of order in international public life, urged a proportionate and discriminate use of armed force against Saddam Hussein took on a moral responsibility for their actions—which included, inescapably, the killing of innocents. But it should also be understood that those who rejected the use of military force were not absolved from moral responsibility for what would have followed had their counsel been taken, which would have included the killing of innocents, and in large numbers. The gruesome stories of what was going on in Kuwait while we were "giving sanctions a chance" should have made that clear, and beyond reasonable argument.

Amid all the talk of a "new world order," it is well to remember Albert Camus's challenge to men of conscience in the immediate aftermath of the Second World War: the task, Camus wrote, was to create an international order in which decent men might be "neither victims nor executioners."[36] That remains a noble goal. It is not a goal that embodies the fullness of "peace" in Christian theology. But it is fully congruent with classic Christian understandings of peace as *tranquillitas ordinis*. It is a goal America's religious institutions might well take as their own.

PART THREE

Key Documents

1. Message and Resolution From the Executive Coordinating Committee of the National Council of Churches

This message, to member communions, and resolution were adopted by the Executive Coordinating Committee of the National Council of the Churches of Christ in the U.S.A. on September 14, 1990.

On August 4, 1990, following Iraq's invasion of Kuwait, the General Secretary of the National Council of the Churches of Christ in the U.S.A. issued a statement expressing its opposition to the invasion and calling for the immediate and speedy withdrawal of Iraqi forces from Kuwait. In the intervening weeks, Iraq has announced its annexation of Kuwait, and the U.S. has sent military forces into the area. The United Nations Security Council has approved resolutions calling for economic sanctions against Iraq and authorizing minimal use of force to enforce those sanctions.

The invasion of Kuwait and succeeding events have created a new and acute refugee problem in the region, with the largest burden falling on the Kingdom of Jordan. Currently there are an estimated 105,000 displaced persons in Jordan. In addition to humanitarian efforts by United Nations agencies, the Middle East Council of Churches has appealed for our prayers and for food, medical supplies, tents and bedding for this increasingly desperate population. The NCCC/USA's unit for Church World Service and Witness has, in turn, appealed for $75,000 to assist the MECC in its relief efforts.

Iraq's Invasion and Attempted Annexation of Kuwait

In response to Iraq's invasion of Kuwait on 2 August 1990, the General Secretary of the National Council of the Churches of Christ in the U.S.A. issued a statement which strongly opposed that invasion. The Executive Coordinating Committee of the NCCC/USA reaffirms the content of that statement.

Subsequently Iraq has illegally annexed Kuwait, basing its actions on historical claims to Kuwaiti territory and on the unrepresentative character of the Kuwaiti government. It has also accused Kuwait of inappropriate production and pricing of its oil. The invasion and annexation of Kuwait has been widely condemned by the international community. While it is true that national boundaries in the Middle East are a legacy of the colonial period, alterations of the boundaries of nation-states may not, under international law, be undertaken through unilateral military action. Neither the nature of a particular government nor its economic policies can be taken as a justification for external intervention. Iraq's own recent history of political repression and unrepresentative rule give its claims an especially hollow ring.

The NCCC/USA supports the United Nations Security Council in its call for the application of economic sanctions against Iraq as a means of inducing the withdrawal of Iraqi forces from Kuwait. Such concerted nonviolent efforts on the part of the international community and particularly of the Arab states offer the best hope for a fair resolution of this issue.

The U.S. Response

The rapid military response of the U.S. government to this crisis, in consultation with Saudi Arabia and other governments, is widely perceived to have deterred further Iraqi incursions. However, the growing magnitude of the U.S. military presence and the apparent open-ended nature of the

U.S. involvement in the region give rise to serious questions which we believe the churches should consider with care. The extent of the commitment of U.S. forces and weaponry in the Gulf region is the largest U.S. military deployment since the Vietnam War. The possibility that some U.S. troops and much of this weaponry may remain in the region does not bode well for the future peace of the region particularly in light of the fact that the Middle East's political disputes remain unresolved. It is the open-ended nature of the U.S. commitment of troops and the long-term intentions of the U.S. with regard to a permanent military presence in the Gulf that should be the subject of open debate.

We are also concerned by the extent to which this introduction of military forces is perceived to be a unilateral U.S. action, despite President Bush's assertion that the U.S. is acting under the authority conveyed by U.N. Security Council resolutions. We believe that all efforts to implement U.N. Security Council resolutions ought to be carried out under the aegis of the U.N. Similarly, international resources which have been garnered in response to U.S. appeals ought to be directed to the United Nations peacekeeping effort.

We are further concerned about the lack of clarity regarding the goals of this deployment of forces. Is the goal the restoration of the *status quo ante bellum*? Will U.S. intervention assure the return of the ruling family to power in Kuwait? Will the U.S. seek to guarantee the Kuwaitis' right to self-determination and representative government? Or is the goal of this military action preeminently the protection of U.S. access to oil supplies? We believe that the U.S. should act not primarily out of its interest in oil and power, but in response to the aspirations of the people of the Middle East for development, justice, peace, and accountable government.

Humanitarian Issues

We are keenly aware of the humanitarian dimensions of this crisis. Hundreds of thousands of expatriate workers have been compelled to leave Iraq and Kuwait, most of them seeking refuge in Jordan. Many of these people arrived malnourished and ill, having been exposed to the elements. They are the most numerous and the most desperate of the victims of this crisis. We intend to respond generously to the appeal issued by the Middle East Council of Churches for food, medicine and bedding to meet the most immediate needs of these displaced persons. Further, we shall urge the U.S. government to make a generous contribution to the appeal issued by the International Organization for Migration (IOM) to enable the airlift of evacuees stranded in Jordan.

In light of past experience, the international community has elaborated strict codes of humanitarian law in the case of armed conflict. We are concerned that these norms are being widely ignored. For example, the detention by Iraq of civilians and their use as "shields" is an open violation of these standards of conduct. The Iraqi government should expedite their immediate and safe return to their countries of origin. On the same humanitarian grounds we deplore Iraq's confiscation and appropriation of Kuwaiti foodstuffs and medical supplies.

We are also deeply concerned about Iraqi civilians. In accordance with Security Council Resolution 660 and subsequent clarification by the Security Council, we believe that essential foodstuffs and medical supplies should not be included in the embargo against Iraq. Consistent with the long-standing policies of the churches regarding humanitarian aid, we would oppose any attempt on the part of the United States or any other government to withhold food or medical supplies for political purposes.

Wider Implications

This crisis has an impact on the region as a whole. Although there seems to be no unanimity of opinion, for many Middle Easterners the introduction of U.S. forces into the region provokes bitter historical memories of past Western interventions in the Middle East. The prompt and massive response on the part of the U.S. to this particular crisis, and the U.S. support of the U.N. Security Council resolutions relating to this crisis, stand in sharp contrast to U.S. negligence regarding the implementation of U.N. Security Council resolutions 242 and 338, which call for the withdrawal of Israeli troops from the territories occupied in the 1967 War and the convening of an international conference to resolve the Israeli-Palestinian issue. We believe that a comprehensive and nonviolent approach to the region's issues, under the auspices of the United Nations, offers the best hope for future peace with justice in the Middle East.

But the implications of this crisis are not limited to the Middle East. The current crisis also highlights the extent to which the relative affluence of our lifestyle has been dependent on access to inexpensive sources of energy. The ecological crisis and the prospect of conflict over access to oil should encourage us to examine critically and to alter our wasteful and irresponsible stewardship of the gifts of the earth.

In the wake of the hopeful diplomatic events of the past year, some are arguing that we are moving from a dangerous and confrontational bipolar world to a unipolar world in which the U.S. plays the leading role. The current crisis reminds us that we are inevitably a part of a multipolar world of societies in search of a healthy interdependence, an interdependence that is based on mutual respect and a common quest for justice.

The NCCC/USA commends this message to the churches, all Christians, and persons of other faith, urging continuing prayer for peace and justice in the Middle East and to prayerful reflection on the issues raised in this message.

Resolution Regarding the Gulf Crisis

The Executive Coordinating Committee of the National Council of the Churches of Christ in the U.S.A.

1. Urges all governments to comply with all resolutions of the United Nations Security Council dealing with the situation in the Middle East.

2. Urges the U.S. government to contribute generously to United Nations efforts to meet the humanitarian needs of those who have been victimized by the Iraqi invasion of Kuwait and its aftermath and to the International Organization for Migration in its efforts to enable the airlift of evacuees from Jordan.

3. Urges, in accordance with U.N. Security Council resolution 660, that the provision of essential foodstuffs and medicine to civilian populations, including the Iraqi civilian population, be excluded from the economic embargo against Iraq as authorized by the U.N. Security Council.

4. Urges that all U.S. efforts to resolve the current conflict in the Gulf region be undertaken within the framework established by the relevant U.N. Security Council resolutions and that efforts be made as soon as possible to place all foreign military forces under United Nations command.

5. Expresses its opposition to any long-term commitment of U.S. military forces in the Middle East outside the framework of a U.N. peacekeeping force.

2. *Letter From Archbishop Mahony to Secretary of State Baker*

On November 7, 1990, Archbishop Roger M. Mahony of Los Angeles, chairman of the International Policy Committee of the United States Catholic Conference, sent this letter to Secretary of State James A. Baker III. The United States Catholic Conference is the public policy agency of the Roman Catholic bishops of the United States. On November 12 the U.S. bishops, at their annual meeting in Washington, voted to adopt Archbishop Mahony's letter as their own.

I WRITE AS chairman of the International Policy Committee of the U.S. Catholic Conference to share several concerns and criteria regarding possible use of U.S. military force in the Persian Gulf. As Catholic bishops we are deeply concerned about the human consequences of the crisis — the lives already lost or those that could be lost in a war, the freedom denied to hostages, the victims of aggression and the many families divided by the demands of military service. As religious teachers, we are concerned about the moral dimensions of the crisis — the need to resist brutal aggression, to protect the innocent, to pursue both justice and peace, as well as the ethical criteria for the use of force. As U.S. citizens, we are concerned about how our nation can best protect human life and human rights and secure a peaceful and just resolution to the crisis.

Our conference has thus far emphasized five basic issues in addressing the crisis:

1. The clear need to resist aggression. We cannot permit nations to simply overwhelm others by brutal use of force.

2. The need for broad-based, international solidarity which seeks effective and peaceful means to halt and reverse aggression. We strongly support the U.N. actions and the international pressure which has effectively halted Iraqi aggression and offers hope for the peaceful liberation of Kuwait.

3. The need to condemn the taking of hostages and the mistreatment and killing of civilians. We deplore the cynical and intolerable actions of the Iraqi government in taking innocent civilians against their will and using them for protection or propaganda, as well as the brutal treatment of civilians in Kuwait.

4. The essential need to distinguish between the leaders of Iraq and the civilians of Iraq and Kuwait. In the carrying out of the embargo and other actions, we need to take care so that innocent civilians are not deprived of those essentials for the maintenance of life, i.e., food and medicines.

5. The imperative to seek a peaceful resolution of the crisis and pursue legitimate objectives by non-violent diplomatic means. We continue to call for effective solidarity, perseverance and patience in the search for a peaceful and just outcome to the crisis.

It is on this last point, the persistent pursuit of a peaceful solution, that I write to you now. As the Administration assesses the military and geopolitical implications of initiating combat, we also ask you to carefully assess the moral consequences of resort to war.

Our country needs an informed and substantive discussion of the human and ethical dimensions of the policy choices under consideration. In the Catholic community there is a long history of ethical reflection on these issues and diverse points of view. As chairman of this committee, I share these reflections with you, not to offer a definitive judgment but to suggest some essential values and raise some key questions which must be considered as the United States explores its options. We hope they will contribute to the necessary and growing public debate about whether the use of military force could be morally justified and under what, if any, conditions. We specifically seek to draw attention to the ethical dimensions of these choices so that they are not ignored or neglected in a focus on simply military and geopolitical considerations.

In our tradition, while the use of force is not ruled out absolutely, there is a clear presumption against war. The right to self-defense or to repel aggression is restricted and governed by a series of moral principles, often called the "just war" theory. These criteria spell out the conditions which have to be met for war to be morally permissible. Among the major criteria are:

(a) *Just cause*: Is there "a real and certain danger" which can only be confronted by war? Several objectives have been put forth for U.S. policy: to deter and repel aggression, to safeguard human rights, to assure adequate and affordable energy supplies, to advance a new international order, to overthrow a hostile dictator. In order to meet the just cause criteria, U.S. policy would have to clarify its precise objectives, measure them by ethical values and demonstrate that they can only be achieved through the use of force.

(b) *Competent authority*: This principle asks who in this case is the competent authority to authorize the use of force. The president acting alone, the president and Congress, the United Nations, which has played an indispensable role in securing international condemnation of Iraq? This principle is crucial given past conflicts in our own country about who has such powers.

(c) *Right intention*: Are the reasons set forth as a just cause for war the actual objectives of military action?

(d) *Last resort*: Have all peaceful alternatives been fully pursued before war is undertaken? Can the international economic and political pressure on Iraq bring about a just solution over time without resort to violence?

(e) *Probability of success*: Is the prospect of success sufficiently clear to justify the human and other costs of military action?

(f) *Proportionality*: Are the damage to be inflicted and the costs incurred by war proportionate to the objectives to be achieved by taking up arms? In this case are the expressed values at stake so important, i.e., the survival of Kuwait, repelling aggression, etc., that they justify the resort to force and the consequences of the use of force? Will war with Iraq leave the people of Kuwait, the Middle East and the world better or worse off?

In addition to these criteria, there are others which govern the conduct of war. These principles include proportionality and discrimination, i.e., the *military* means used must be commensurate with the evil to be overcome and must be directed at the aggressors, not innocent people. For example, the Second Vatican Council declared, "Any act of war aimed indiscriminately at the destruction of entire cities or of extensive areas along with their population is a crime against God and man himself. It merits unequivocal and unhesitating condemnation."

Military action against Iraq would have to be restrained by these two principles, necessarily ruling out tactics and strategies which could clearly target civilian lives. This means this war would have to be a limited war, raising again the probability of success and the price to be paid given the hostile physical environment, the fragility of the anti-Iraq alliance and the volatility of regional and domestic political support.

These considerations lead me to strongly urge that the United States, in continued cooperation with the United Nations, the Soviet Union, Arab states and other nations, stay the course of persistent, peaceful and determined pressure against Iraq. A resort to war in violation of these criteria would jeopardize many lives, raise serious moral questions and undermine the international solidarity against Iraq. We understand that a strong military presence can give credibility to a vigorous pursuit of non-violent solutions to the crisis. They may also open the door for a new, broader and more imaginative dialogue concerning the deep-seated and long-standing problems which have contributed to the current situation.

We pray for the safety and welfare of the peoples of that troubled region. We pray for the liberation of the hostages and the people of Kuwait. We pray that the American men and women deployed in the Gulf may by their presence support a peaceful resolution of the crisis and return home safely and soon. And finally, we pray that our leaders and all other parties concerned will have the persistence, wisdom and skill to resolve the current crisis in peace and with justice.

3. Message and Resolution From the General Board of the National Council of Churches

This statement was adopted by the General Board of the National Council of the Churches of Christ in the U.S.A. on November 15, 1990.

THE MESSAGE

Theological and Moral Imperative

I, therefore, the prisoner in the Lord, beg you to lead a life worthy of the calling to which you have been called, with all humility and gentleness, with patience, bearing with one another in love, making every effort to maintain the unity of the Spirit in the bonds of peace. (Ephesians 4: 1–3)

THROUGHOUT the history of the church, the question of the admissibility of war as a means of resolving disputes has been a source of differences, and at times division, in the body of Christ. Among our own communions, there is a wide diversity of approaches to this question. For all Christians, however, war is a sign of the sinful human condition, of human alienation from God, of alienation between human beings who are all children of God.

We stand at a unique moment in human history, when all around us seemingly impregnable walls are being broken down and deep historical enmities are being healed. And yet, ironically, at such a moment, our own nation seems to be poised at the brink of war in the Middle East. "What then are we to say about these things?" (Romans 8:31)

The quest for peace and the quest for Christian unity, which is the very reason for our existence as a Council, are intimately related. As churches seeking to recover our unity, we are called to be the salt and leaven of our societies. Together with other faith communities, we are called to address moral and spiritual dimensions in the debate on a national policy that seems to be careening toward war. Believing that Christ is our peace, we cannot do other than to strive to be the incarnation of creation's cry for peace.

Unanswered Questions

Two months ago, on September 14, 1990, the Executive Coordinating Committee of the National Council of the Churches of Christ in the U.S.A. addressed a message to its member communions on the Gulf crisis [see document 1 in this section]. That message condemned Iraq's invasion and occupation of Kuwait, raised serious questions about the decision of the U.S. government to send troops to the Gulf region and about the growing magnitude of U.S. presence, noting that the extent of the commitment of U.S. forces and weaponry was the largest since the Vietnam War. Since then, the U.S. has more than doubled the number of troops sent to the region to a number approaching a half million persons.

The message also questioned the apparent open-ended nature of U.S. military involvement in the Middle East and the failure on the part of the administration clearly to state its goals. President Bush and administration officials have done little to clarify either of those points. Indeed the rationales offered for the steady expansion of U.S. presence have often been misleading and sometimes even contradictory. Early statements that U.S. forces had been deployed for the defense of Saudi Arabia or the enforcement of U.N. sanctions have been supplanted by suggestions of broader goals, including expulsion of Iraqi forces from Kuwait by military means, or even offensive action against Iraq itself. The nation still has not been told in clear and certain terms what would be required for the withdrawal of U.S. troops.

The Prospect of War

The initial response of the NCCC/USA was carefully measured, recognizing the magnitude of the injustice inflicted by Iraq against Kuwait, and the unprecedented reliance by the United States on the mechanisms of the U.N. In contrast, the U.S. administration increasingly prepares for war, a war that could lead to the loss of tens of thousands of lives and the devastation of the region. Such talk has given rise to widespread speculation in our country, in the Middle East and elsewhere that the United States will initiate war.

In the face of such reckless rhetoric and imprudent behavior, as representatives of churches in the United States we feel that we have a moral responsibility publicly and unequivocally to oppose actions that could have such dire consequences.

The Wider Implications

Our earlier message also pointed out that the active U.S. effort to implement United Nations Security Council resolutions relating to the occupation of Kuwait by Iraq stands in marked contrast to U.S. negligence regarding the implementation of Security Council resolutions 242 and 338. These call for the withdrawal of Israeli troops from the territories occupied in the 1967 War and the convening of an international conference to resolve the Israeli-Palestinian issue. There has also been negligence regarding the implementation of Security Council resolutions 359, 360 and 361 which call for the withdrawal "without delay" of Turkish troops from Cyprus and solving the problems of the island through negotiations.

During the intervening weeks the situation in the Israeli-Occupied Territories has, in fact, worsened. The U.S. government's condemnation of the massacre on the Haram al-Sharif/Temple Mount and its endorsement of a U.S. mission to the Occupied Territories was a welcome departure from past policies. The failure of the U.S. government to take any substantive measures to oppose the Israeli occupation, however, weakens the effect of its appropriate outrage over Iraqi aggression against Kuwait. The region cries out for a U.S. policy that seeks to redress all cases of injustice, including those of Israel and Palestine, Lebanon and Cyprus.

The Dangers of Militarization

The presence of U.S. troops in the Middle East has led to an expansion of the military capacity of an already grossly over-militarized region. The proposed billions of dollars of arms sales to Saudi Arabia, the forgiveness of military debts to Egypt and Israel and the supplying of both with new and more sophisticated weaponry, combined with a seeming lack of initiative to resolve the region's unsettled disputes, can only be seen as morally irresponsible.

The Price of War

The price of war and the preparation for further conflict is already being paid in human terms. Hundreds of thousands of foreign workers and their families have been compelled to leave Kuwait and Iraq, creating enormous strains on the Kingdom of Jordan and the Republic of Egypt and, ultimately, on the societies to which they are returning.

The cost of the current U.S. military presence in the Gulf is estimated at $1 billion per month. This "extra-budgetary expenditure" is once again likely to reduce further the nation's capacity to address human needs in our own society. Thus, among the early victims of this tragic engagement will certainly be the growing number of the poor, homeless, sick and elderly. The corrosive effects on our own nation will be felt especially by racial ethnic communities who make up a disproportionate number both of the poor and those who are on the front lines of military confrontation.

We are appalled by the past and present behavior of the regime in Iraq, one which has previously enjoyed U.S. support. But the demonization of the Iraqi people and their leader has led to an increased incidence of defamation of or discrimination against persons of Arab descent or appearance.

A New World Order

We stand on the threshold of a "new world order." Indeed, the near unanimous condemnation by the nations of the world of Iraq's illegal occupation of its neighbor, Kuwait, shows the promise of a new approach to the vocation of peacemaking for which the United Nations was created forty-five years ago. There are present in this moment seeds either of a new era of international cooperation under the rule of international law or of rule based upon superior power, which holds the prospect of continuing dehumanizing chaos.

Our churches have long sought to nurture and bring to fruition the seeds of hope. The power we would invoke is not the power of the gun, nor is it the power of wealth and affluence; we would invoke the power of the cross and the resurrection, symbols for us of love and hope. As Christians in the U.S. we must witness against weak resignation to the illogical pursuit of militarism and war. We must witness to our belief in the capacity of human beings and human societies to seek and achieve reconciliation.

The General Board of the NCCC/USA commends this message to the churches, all Christians, and persons of other faiths, inviting them to join us in continuing prayer and urgent action to avert war in the Persian/Arabian Gulf region, and to join in the quest for a just and a durable peace in the Middle East.

Resolution on the Gulf and Middle East Crisis

The General Board of the National Council of Churches, meeting in Portland, Oregon, November 14–16, 1990, recognizing its solidarity with the Christians of the Middle East and with the Middle East Council of Churches,

Urges the government of Iraq to release immediately all those citizens of other nations being held against their will in Kuwait or Iraq and to withdraw immediately its troops and occupation forces from Kuwait.

Calls for the continued rigorous application of the sanctions against Iraq authorized by the United Nations Security Council until such time as it withdraws its forces from Kuwait.

Reiterates its opposition to the withholding of food and medicine as a weapon against civilian populations.

Encourages the Secretary General of the United Nations to exercise fully his own good offices in pursuit of a rapid negotiated resolution of the present conflict in the Gulf.

Calls upon the President and U.S. Congress to pursue every means for a negotiated political solution to the crisis in the Gulf, including direct negotiations with Iraq.

Reiterates support for the convening under U.N. auspices of an international conference for a comprehensive peace in the Middle East, as a means of implementing United Nations Security Council resolutions on Israel and Palestine, Lebanon and Cyprus, recognizing that the present crisis cannot be isolated from the unresolved issues of the region as a whole.

Calls for an immediate halt to the buildup and the withdrawal of U.S. troops from the Gulf region except those which might be required and explicitly recommended by the Security

Council of the United Nations in accordance with the relevant provisions of the United Nations Charter.

Calls upon the U.S. government to give leadership to the institution of an immediate and complete embargo under U.N. auspices on arms transfers to the Middle East.

Calls upon member communions, congregations, local and regional ecumenical agencies and individuals to make peace in the Middle East a paramount and urgent priority for prayer, study and action.

Expresses its profound gratitude for the witness of the Middle East Council of Churches and commits itself to continued partnership with the MECC in its efforts for peace, justice and development.

Requests the President and General Secretary to engage in dialogue and to coordinate where possible and appropriate with the National Conference of Catholic Bishops and Evangelical organizations with regard to the development of statements or actions in a effort to provide a common Christian witness.

Requests the President and General Secretary to communicate this resolution to the President and Secretary of State, to the members of Congress, to the President of Iraq, to the Secretary General of the United Nations, the World Council of Churches, and to the Middle East Council of Churches.

4. *Letter From Archbishop Pilarczyk to President Bush*

On November 15, 1990, Archbishop Daniel Pilarczyk of Cincinnati, president of the National Conference of Catholic Bishops, sent the following letter to President Bush. The letter reflected the discussion on the Gulf crisis by some 300 bishops meeting in a closed-door executive session on November 14.

I WRITE AS president of the National Conference of Catholic Bishops to offer our prayers for you, our president, at this time of difficult choices on how best to confront aggression and preserve human life and human rights in the Middle East. I also write to share our conference's deep concerns about the moral dangers and human costs which could be the result of war in the Persian Gulf.

The Catholic bishops of the United States met in our nation's capital this week and voted to affirm and make their own the enclosed letter of Archbishop Roger Mahony sent to Secretary Baker on November 7. The letter's central point was the urgent need to assess carefully and thoroughly the ethical and human consequences of war in the Persian Gulf. The letter strongly urges the moral imperative of persistent pursuit of non-violent international pressure to halt and reverse Iraq's aggression without resort to war. [See document 2.]

As pastors we are deeply concerned about the human consequences of the crisis—the lives already lost or those that could be lost in war, the freedom denied to hostages, the suffering of victims of aggression and the many families separated by the demands of military service. As religious teachers, we are concerned about the moral dimensions of the crisis — the need to resist aggression, to protect the innocent, to pursue both justice and peace in a way that conforms with ethical criteria for the use of force. As U.S. citizens, we are concerned how our nation can best protect human life and human rights and secure a peaceful and just resolution to the crisis.

These are not new concerns for Catholic bishops. We are heirs of a long tradition of thought and moral reflection on issues of war and peace, including "The Challenge of Peace," our pastoral letter of 1983. Catholic teaching reflects a strong presumption against war while admitting the moral permissibility of the use of force under certain restrictive conditions. These traditional "just war" criteria limit strictly the circumstances under which war may be morally justifiable and also govern the means by which war may be carried out. Now our conference seeks to apply this tradition to the complex and changing situation in the Persian Gulf. While there may be diverse points of view on the specific application of these principles, our conference finds significant consensus on four key priorities:

1. Strong condemnation of Iraq's aggression, hostage taking and other violations of human rights and our strong support for worldwide peaceful pressure and action to deter Iraq's aggression and secure the peaceful liberation of Kuwait.

2. The urgent need for the careful consideration of the moral and human consequences of the use of force as well as the military and political implications.

3. Clear moral criteria must be met to justify the use of military force. As outlined in Archbishop Mahony's letter, these include questions of a clear and just cause for war, proper authority and sufficient probability of success to justify the human and other costs of military action. The criteria also ask whether war is genuinely a last resort; all reasonable

peaceful alternatives must be fully pursued. Another criterion is proportionality: The human, economic and other costs of war must be proportionate to the objective to be achieved by the use of weapons of war. In this case, will war with Iraq leave the people of Kuwait, the Middle East and the world better or worse off? Our tradition also requires that the means and weapons used to pursue war must be proportionate as well and must discriminate between combatants and ordinary civilians. I fear that, in this situation, moving beyond the deployment of military forces in an effort to deter Iraqi aggression to the undertaking of offensive military action could well violate those criteria, especially the principles of proportionality and last resort.

4. Therefore, in our conference's view, our nation should continue strong, persistent and determined international and peaceful pressure against Iraq. Our conference understands that a strong military presence can give credibility to a vigorous pursuit of diplomatic and economic approaches to the crisis. Our concern is that the pressures to use military force could grow as the pursuit of non-violent options almost inevitably becomes difficult, complex and slow. We urge our government and our allies to continue to pursue the course of peaceful pressure and not resort to war. The use of weapons of war cannot be a substitute for the difficult, often time-consuming and frustrating work of searching for political solutions to the deep-seated problems in the Middle East which have contributed to this current crisis.

We are also concerned not only about the international consequences of possible war, but the domestic impact as well: the resources diverted, the human needs neglected, the potential political conflict and divisions within our society.

I believe, Mr. President, these are your concerns, even as they are ours.

I offer these reflections not to diminish in any way the necessary condemnation of Iraq's brutal actions. Rather, I speak with the firm conviction that our nation needs to continue to assess and discuss the ethical dimensions of this difficult situation. These discussions and this assessment must take place before, not after, offensive action is taken.

We stand with our government and the United Nations in the effort to halt and reverse Iraqi aggression, to condemn the taking of hostages and to secure their release. We strongly support and commend your efforts to build global solidarity and worldwide pressure against Iraq. Because of the serious moral and human factors involved, we ask you and the leaders of other governments to continue and intensify the determined and creative pursuit of a peaceful solution that seeks to bring justice to the region without resort to war.

Our prayers are with you as you face these awesome challenges and as you undertake a journey this Thanksgiving season so important for our country and the world. We also pray that other world leaders meet their responsibilities to pursue both justice and peace. Our prayers also go out to all those directly touched by this crisis: the victims of aggression, the hostages, troops in the field and their families.

We especially remember the members of our military forces, who face a difficult task in trying circumstances and who will bear the burden of the decisions made on how best to resolve this crisis. We hope and pray that these reflections from our conference's perspective as pastors and teachers will strengthen our nation's determination to pursue true justice through peaceful means.

5. *Testimony of Archbishop Roach Before a Senate Committee*

Archbishop John R. Roach of St. Paul–Minneapolis, the successor to Archbishop Roger Mahony as chairman of the United States Catholic Conference International Policy Committee, presented the following testimony on behalf of the conference to the Senate Foreign Relations Committee on December 6, 1990.

I COME BEFORE this committee on behalf of the U.S. Catholic Conference, the public-policy agency of the Roman Catholic bishops of the United States, to share our profound concerns about the moral dangers and human costs which could be the result of war in the Middle East. In this testimony, I seek to share the recent statement of our bishops's conference and to address three issues: (1) the significance, politically and morally, of the public debate in the United States; (2) the moral criteria which should inform, direct and guide our discussion and decision-making on the use of force in the Middle East; and (3) some application of these moral criteria in the current crisis.

Role and Reflections of the Bishops' Conference

At the outset, let me address directly the question of why Catholic bishops are speaking out on this complex, controversial and conflicted matter. We recognize quite clearly that we are not experts on military or geopolitical matters. We are, however, pastors and teachers and citizens in a nation considering whether to go to war. As pastors, we are deeply concerned about the human consequences of this crisis—the lives lost or damaged by Iraq's aggression, the many lives that could be lost in war, the freedom denied to hostages and victims of aggression, and the families disrupted by the military steps already taken. As moral and religious teachers, we are required to address the moral dimensions of the choices facing our nation—the urgent need to resist aggression, to protect human life, to pursue both justice and peace, and to weigh the moral dangers and human costs of war. As U.S. citizens, we hope our nation will use its power and resources to restore justice while pursuing peace.

These are not new concerns for us. We are heirs of a long tradition of thought and reflection on these issues. Silence in this situation would be an abandonment of our responsibilities as pastors, teachers and religious leaders. We hope our reflections will contribute to a broad and necessary public dialogue about how our nation can best defend human rights and protect human life at this dangerous moment.

We very much welcome and support the president's announcement of a week ago that a direct dialogue with Iraq will be undertaken to make clear the world's insistence that Iraq abandon its aggression and to explore a peaceful resolution of the crisis. We hope this important step will contribute in a decisive way to a solution that is both just and peaceful. I commend the president for this decision and pray that this major step forward will succeed in securing the liberation of Kuwait. This welcome initiative, however, does not relieve us of the urgent responsibility or necessity of a rigorous and informed analysis of under what conditions the use of deadly force can be justified. The success or failure of any particular diplomatic initiative cannot be the determining factor in the decision to go to war. We still must meet the traditional moral tests to justify resort to war.

At our recent general meeting, we Catholic bishops set aside our planned agenda to address the crisis in the Persian Gulf. We voted overwhelmingly (249–14) to make our own the attached letter of our International Policy Committee to Secretary of State James Baker [see document 2] outlining a series of moral questions about the use of force. And later, after discussion by the bishops in both public and executive session, the president of the bishops' conference, Archbishop Daniel Pilarczyk, wrote the attached letter to President Bush [see document 4] urging "the moral imperative of persistent pursuit of non-violent international pressure to halt and reverse Iraq's aggression without resort to war."

In that letter, Archbishop Pilarczyk describes several areas of consensus for our conference:

1. Universal condemnation of Iraq's brutal aggression and hostage taking.

2. Strong support for the worldwide peaceful pressure to deter and reverse Iraq's aggression.

3. The urgent need to consider fully the moral and human consequences of the use of force and to apply traditional moral criteria to the situation in the gulf.

4. The conviction that our nation should continue to apply strong, persistent and determined pressure to Iraq without resort to offensive military action, which could well violate traditional moral criteria.

These letters are the foundation of my testimony today. The efforts of the Catholic conference are attempts to define and raise the central moral questions which ought to be asked and answered whenever a nation stands at the intersection of war and peace as the United States does today. I address these difficult questions to prompt serious reflection, not to provide easy answers. There is a diversity of views within both our religious community and the wider society on the specific application of moral principles. But I hope these questions can help clarify both the ends we seek and the means we choose in pursuing justice in this difficult situation.

Significance and Substance of the Public Debate

In his letter to Secretary Baker, Archbishop Mahony, my predecessor as chairman of our International Policy Committee, said, "Our country needs an informed and substantive discussion of the human and ethical dimensions of the policy choices under consideration." The current policy choices concern how best to respond to the aggression perpetuated by Iraq against Kuwait, its territory, its sovereignty and its people. The American people and the Catholic bishops are united in our condemnation of Saddam Hussein's brutal action against Kuwait and the profound threat it poses to the very concept of international order. The difficult question is not whether Iraq's action should be opposed, but how best to do it.

The significance of the already wide-ranging public discussion taking place in the United States is that we have a rare public moment when the choice between war and peace, and when the merits and consequences of the use of force can be explicitly considered and debated.

The very scope and intensity of the debate under way, one which includes congresspersons and columnists, current and former public officials, religious leaders and military experts, relatives of those now deployed in the Gulf and those held hostage, illustrates a basic point: The moment of decision on the offensive use of force is still ahead of us. There is no clear U.S. consensus at the moment to sustain a resort to war. More time is clearly needed to consider the alternatives to and consequences of war. There should be no rush to judgment on the fateful question of turning from sustained political and economic pressure on Saddam Hussein to deciding there is no road left but war.

Some fear that public debate on the wisdom, morality or effectiveness of various options can send a confused or wrong signal to Saddam Hussein. I believe disciplined, reasoned public debate can send a much different message: that our nation will not tolerate aggression, that hostage taking and the exploitation of hostages will not be effective, and that the broad coalition of nations skillfully woven together by the Bush administration has the means and the will to oppose successfully Iraq's aggression. A discussion about appropriate means should not be confused with a debate about ultimate ends. This debate is about which means can be both effective in opposing aggression and consistent with our moral values as a people.

Some also warn that this kind of discussion can undermine the explicit military threat that is being made in order to force Iraq to back down and that this kind of public debate could make war more likely. However, the serious danger with this approach is that our nation could find itself fighting a war without clarity of purpose, public and political consensus, or adequate moral justification. The decision on whether we go to war should be made by our nation with full discussion of the moral, military, and other dimensions, not by Iraq's refusal to respond to deadlines. We need to examine thoroughly the moral and human consequences of war before, not after, offensive action is chosen.

In this public debate we should examine each of the relevant political, strategic, and economic issues at stake; but we must test them all in light of moral criteria. These moral questions probe the human costs and consequences of the use of force. There are heavy costs when aggression occurs; and there are also heavy costs when war is used to oppose aggression. The challenge before us is to redress the injustice which has occurred and to do it—if at all possible—without the use of deadly force. Some say war is already inevitable; I say that is much too quick a judgment and far too simple a solution. War could make the situation worse, not better. In order to avoid quick, simple and possibly wrong answers, we should test these proposals against the moral questions, principles and criteria which have been developed over the ages to assess the use of deadly force.

Moral Criteria

A. *The Catholic Church and the Ethic of War and Peace*: In our teaching about war and peace, the Catholic Church seeks to lift up these moral dimensions, ethical consequences and human costs. In our tradition, moral reasoning about the relationship of politics and war begins with a presumption against the use of force. Even though the ethic which I represent as a Catholic bishop has been called the just war tradition, its purpose is not to facilitate the choice for war, but to make that choice both difficult and rarely used. This moral vision does allow, in very restricted cases, a justifiable resort to force. In the twentieth century, however, developments in weaponry have consistently raised the standards for justifying force and thereby reduced the instances where moral approval can be given to the option of war. Modern warfare, even in its conventional version, is very hard to justify morally. Therefore, we begin our public debate about the Gulf with a presumption against going to war.

If the presumption is to be overridden or reversed three general questions must be asked and answered: (1) Why can force be used—for what cause? (2) When can forced be used—under what conditions? (3) How should force be used—by what methods and means? These three questions in turn yield the specific criteria of the just war ethic that have developed in our tradition and are reflected in our letter to Secretary Baker.[1]

---

[1]In his letter, Archbishop Mahony outlines the just war criteria in this way: "(a) Just Cause: Is there a 'real and certain danger' which can only be confronted by war? Several objectives have been put forth for U.S. policy: to deter and repel aggression, to safeguard human rights, to assure adequate and affordable energy supplies, to advance a new international order, to overthrow a hostile dictator. In order to meet the just cause criteria U.S. policy would have to clarify its precise objectives, measure them by ethical

B. *Just Cause*: The why question focuses upon the purpose for which force may be used, the question of just cause. Only the most severe circumstances can justify the use of deadly force. Generally speaking, our moral tradition has judged that force can be used to protect the innocent from attack, to restore rights wrongfully denied and to re-establish order necessary for decent human existence.

Since August, the United States has articulated a series of purposes or objectives for U.S. policy. I believe it is necessary to sort out and test these objectives. They are not of the same value, and they do not all qualify as objectives for which the use of force can be an appropriate response. Among the expressed objectives of U.S. policy are the following: (1) to defend Saudi Arabia and to deter aggression against other Arab states; (2) to restore Kuwait's territorial integrity and its government; to expel Iraq from Kuwait and thereby terminate its brutal oppression of the Kuwaiti people; (3) to free all hostages held by Iraq; (4) to contribute to long-term stability in the Middle East by reducing the threat Iraq poses for its neighbors; (5) to guarantee secure access to oil supplies for

---

values and demonstrate that they can only be achieved through the use of force. (b) Competent Authority: This principle asks who in this case is the competent authority to authorize the use of force. The president acting alone, the president and Congress, the United Nations, which has played an indispensable role in securing international condemnation of Iraq? This principle is crucial, given past conflicts in our own country about who has such powers. (c) Right Intention: Are the reasons set forth as a just cause for war the actual objectives of military action? (d) Last Resort: Have all peaceful alternatives been fully pursued before war is undertaken? Can the international economic and political pressure on Iraq bring about a just solution over time without resort to violence? (e) Probability of Success: Is the prospect of success sufficiently clear to justify the human and other costs of military action? (f) Proportionality: Is the damage to be inflicted and the costs incurred by war proportionate to the objectives to be achieved by taking up arms? In this case are the expressed values at stake so important, i.e., the survival of Kuwait, repelling aggression, etc., that they justify the resort to force and the consequences of the use of force? Will war with Iraq leave the people of Kuwait, the Middle East and the world better or worse off?" (November 12, 1990)

the international community; and (6) to prevent Iraq from achieving nuclear capabilities.

It seems useful to note that the longer the list of purposes is, the more difficult it is to achieve either clarity or success. One of the troubling aspects of the current debate is how some commentators turn this extended list of objectives into a series of tests, where all objectives (and others they add like bringing down Saddam Hussein) become the minimum the United States must achieve in the Gulf. The logic of this argument is that failure to achieve all of the above would be seen as a serious defeat for the United States. The dynamic of this analysis almost inevitability leads to the conclusion that the use of deadly force is absolutely necessary for the United States. This multiplication of objectives is troubling, both politically and morally.

In this debate, our nation needs to clarify and assess the actual objectives of U.S. policy and evaluate whether the use of force is essential for their achievement. A quick survey of the most compelling reasons illustrates why there is such a strong public consensus supporting the efforts to resist Iraq's aggression. Iraq's flagrant violation of international law has given the international community good reason to mobilize political opposition, economic sanctions and military forces against Iraq. Still greater clarity on which, if any, of the several causes justify the use of force and whether force is the only effective alternative is needed.

Clarifying and establishing a cause sufficient for the use of force is not adequate justification for war. The why question must lead to the when and how questions. These questions regarding the conditions for justifiable force place restraints on states precisely when they are convinced just cause exists. These questions restrain us when our instinct is to say, in the face of such obvious evil, war must be the only way. These questions remind us that the means of war can easily distort our most well-chosen objectives; that the costs of war are paid by the innocent as well as the guilty; and that the consequences of war are very unpredictable.

C. *Proper Authority, Last Resort and Proportionality*: In this testimony, I concentrate on three central tests which I believe are most pertinent to the present crisis. The application of moral principles to specific questions always involves prudential judgments based on assessments of the empirical situation. I share these reflections in the hope that they contribute to the dialogue over the best choices for our nation.

1. *Proper Authority*: This criterion raises the complex question of the division of power and authority in the U.S. constitutional framework. I am not a constitutional expert, and I do not intend to enter the debate about the scope of presidential authority and the rights of the Congress. However, I would use this principle to make a citizen's point: Where the decision is as fateful as war and peace, we all have an interest in shaping a decision which benefits from the widest range of insight, wisdom and judgment. A possible danger of the moment is that massive mobilization of forces may drive the decision about war and peace to a precipitous conclusion. In this case, it seems that our national interest will best be served by defining "proper authority" in this case broadly, not narrowly. As has been pointed out, a president can start a war, but only a united nation can effectively sustain one.

2. *Last Resort*: The purpose of this principle is to insist that a nation must fully and faithfully pursue (not just try, but fully pursue) all reasonable political, diplomatic and economic means to resist aggression, vindicate rights and secure justice. In the present policy debate, this principle has particular relevance.

In response to the Iraqi invasion, the United States has made five related responses. The first was our leadership role in a series of U.N. resolutions which led to the economic blockade of Iraq and which seek to use non-violent but powerful measures to reverse the invasion and restore the *status quo ante* between Iraq and Kuwait. The second was the initial deployment of 200,000 American troops and the building of a coalition of other forces in order to deter further Iraqi aggression. The third was the decision to dispatch an additional 200,000 U.S. forces and to abandon rotation plans in order to provide an "offensive capacity." The fourth has been the successful effort to secure U.N. approval for what is generally understood as the use of offensive force after January 15. The fifth was the recent announcement of face-to-face discussion between the United States and Iraq.

The last-resort criterion places an enormous burden of proof on those who say it is now time to go to war. While I'm not an expert in these matters, I note that several experienced national leaders have recently testified that war is not the only way to resist this aggression and that non-military options should be given a much longer time to work. The endorsement of the embargo and its potential long-term effectiveness by a number of former military and governmental officials highlights the need to keep in mind this criterion of last resort. The ethical restraint on war requires a nation to try all means short of war. The embargo needs time to work. If appropriate time is not allowed for it to work, it is not accurate to say it has been tried and failed. Last resort requires that the embargo not be dismissed before it has had the time needed to achieve the legitimate objectives for which it was designed. Before war can be justified, all peaceful means must be fully pursued. Thus far, I do not believe the principle of last resort has been met.

3. *Proportionality*: This criterion, I believe, is the most crucial measure of the current debate and is always difficult to apply. When we consider going to war, one question which the history of modern war has taught us to ask is, At what price? Are the objectives to be sought proportionate to the damage to be done and the human costs to be incurred by

war? Are the means to be used consistent with the goals to be sought? In addressing the proportionality question we should particularly ask about (a) the kind of war this could be; (b) the scope of the war we might expect; and (c) the possible outcome of such a war.

(a) The kind of war: Will this war be as swift, neat and clear-cut as some suggest? Will it discriminate between aggressors and innocent civilians? With more than 400,000 allied forces facing over 600,000 Iraqi forces arrayed in the open territory of the Arabian desert and loaded with sophisticated weaponry, can we be certain about theories of a short, decisive battle? The air war, which some advocate as most effective and appropriate, is a war to be waged against an industrial and populous society. Many military targets are located in cities and populated areas. Can we adequately discriminate between civilians and aggressors?

(b) The scope of the war: Can war be confined just to Kuwait and Iraq? This war would be fought in a region laced with interlocking conflicts: Israel vs. Arab; Arab vs. Arab; with long histories of animosity and ancient grudges. It is these concerns and questions which lead me to doubt whether offensive military action can be demonstrated to be a truly proportionate response to the crisis in the Gulf.

(c) The consequences of war: What would we find at the end of the conflict? Of course, we want Iraq to leave Kuwait. But the consequences of war are rarely singular and fine tuned. As our previous letter asks, Will war with Iraq leave the people of Kuwait, the Middle East and the world, better or worse off?

Several leaders have made the point that our response to this crisis will set an important precedent for the post-Cold War period and could help shape a new international order. We agree, and that is why we are so insistent that political and non-violent means be fully pursued in order to deter and reverse aggression. We do not want to set the precedent of war as the logical or necessary response to serious provocation, violations of human rights, economic threats, or nuclear proliferation. The world needs to develop and strengthen its capacity to resist such serious violations of order and justice by united and determined action short of war. Given the remarkable global coalition opposed to Iraq's aggression, the world can demonstrate in this case that justice can be brought about by determined and powerful solidarity among nations to isolate and punish those who violate fundamental principles of international order without launching a war.

Conclusion

In our view, the fundamental moral challenge for the United States and this broad international coalition remains to mobilize effectively the political will, diplomatic skill and economic strength to resist and reverse Iraq's aggression by peaceful, but determined means. We recognize that the deployment of significant military force can enhance the credibility and effectiveness of strong and non-violent pressures. But I believe a resort to offensive military action in this situation could well violate traditional moral criteria, undermine domestic unity and global solidarity against Iraq, and bring about an exceedingly dangerous, divisive, bloody and unnecessary war.

We appreciate the difficult situation our government faces in trying to reverse Iraq's aggression. We commend the skill and commitment the administration has shown in the building of an impressive worldwide coalition against aggression and the vital role of the United Nations in this effort. We recognize that quick U.S. action together with key Arab states and other nations probably deterred further aggression. We very much welcome and commend the recent decision to pursue direct contacts with Iraq and pray for its success. We strongly urge that our government continue to isolate and pressure Iraq by strong but peaceful means without resort to offensive military action. Give the world the time it needs to convince Iraq through non-violent but determined pressure that aggression will not pay.

We urge our nation and the global community to show their resolve, not by resort to war but by determined, steady and persistent pressure that will deny Iraq any advantage from aggression and ultimately require Iraq to respond to the powerful and united voices and actions of the world community. Patience and tenacity are not signs of weakness, but of strength and determination. We believe our nation and the world will continue to unite around the necessity of denying Hussein and his regime any benefit from their aggression. We hope and pray our nation will continue to choose determined and united pressure over the dangerous human and moral consequences of war.

It still seems possible to achieve the necessary objectives of opposing aggression, liberating Kuwait, and defending Saudi Arabia without resort to deadly force. The accomplishment of these goals by political means would be a resounding achievement for U.S. policy and for international order. It is this outcome which I believe should be desired, sought, and prayed for.

6. *Statement From Eighteen Church Leaders to the American People*

A statement entitled "War Is Not the Answer: A Message to the American People" was issued in New York City on December 21, 1990, by eighteen church leaders who participated in a December 14–21 Church Leaders' Peace Pilgrimage to the Middle East. The trip was coordinated by staff members of the National Council of Churches.

WE ARE marching toward war. Indeed the stakes are horribly high. Military experts predict casualties in the tens and hundreds of thousands. And it won't end there. War would unleash a chain of human tragedies that will be with us for generations to come.

Our Christmas pilgrimage to the Middle East has utterly convinced us that war is not the answer. We believe the resort to massive violence to resolve the Gulf crisis would be politically and morally indefensible. One clear message emerged from our many conversations in these holy lands—"war would be a disaster for us all." We were told again and again, "Please go home and tell the American people that a way to peace can and must be found." We have concluded that in the Middle East today it is no longer only a question of right and wrong; it is also a matter of life and death.

The unspeakable loss of lives, especially innocent civilians, would be unacceptable on moral grounds. Nations hold in their hands weapons of mass destruction. It is entirely possible that war in the Middle East will destroy everything. No cause will be served, no crisis resolved, no justice secured.

War will not liberate Kuwait, it will destroy it. War will not save us from weapons of mass destruction, it will unleash them. War will not establish regional stability, it will inflame the entire Middle East. War will not resolve longstanding conflicts, it will explode them wider and deeper. War will not unite the Arabs with the West, it will rekindle painful historical memories of past efforts by the "Christian" West to dominate the "Muslim" East and divide us as never before, with potentially disastrous results for the local Christian communities. War will not stop aggression, it will instead rapidly accelerate the cycle of violence and revenge, which will not be limited to the Middle East.

We will also be ravaged here at home by a war in the Middle East. Given the make-up of U.S. volunteer armed forces, we know that those who will do most of the suffering and dying in the Gulf War will be disproportionately low-income and people of color. Similarly, if "Desert Shield" continues to swallow up limited national resources in a time of economic contraction, the prospects of justice at home will disappear like a mirage in the sand.

Again and again during our pilgrimage we heard the sentiment that peace in the Middle East is indivisible. While we do not accept the proposition that the resolution of all other conflicts must precede the solution of the Gulf crisis, we do believe that there will be no lasting peace in the region until interrelated issues are dealt with in a comprehensive framework. What is required is not "linkage," but consistency in the implementation of U.S. foreign policy. Our government should support the convening of an international Middle East peace conference by the United Nations.

We have prayed in Jerusalem for the peace of Jerusalem. Jerusalem's vocation as the city of peace will not be realized until both Israelis and Palestinians are free and fully protected in the exercise of their human rights within secure and recognized boundaries.

We have seen both the hopes and the frustrations of Lebanon as it emerges from its fifteen-year nightmare of civil war. A durable peace in Lebanon requires the withdrawal of all foreign forces—Syrian, Israeli and Iranian—and international support as Lebanon seeks to rebuild its shattered society.

We have felt the anguish of a divided Cyprus, which seems to have been forgotten by the world community. Cyprus can be united and free only when occupation forces are withdrawn from the island, and a unified and pluralistic Republic of Cyprus is acknowledged as the only legitimate government of the entire island and its population.

There is no such thing as a benign occupation. Occupation of the lands of others is wrong. It breeds frustration and frustration leads to conflict. Even as we oppose the Iraqi occupation of Kuwait on moral grounds, so also we believe that the West Bank and Gaza, Lebanon and Cyprus must be free. These occupations must end before even more precious human blood is shed.

We have looked into the faces of children in Iraq. In Jordan we have witnessed in dusty refugee camps the compassionate response of a democratic government and the churches to the thousands of evacuees who descended upon a country already impoverished by the Gulf crisis. We have seen fear in the eyes of people who could lose their homes or their lives in the event of war.

Having seen the faces of victims and potential victims, we believe that there must be an alternative to war. That alternative is negotiations—serious and substantive negotiations. If the United Nations can be mobilized to impose sanctions and to set dead-lines, it can also be mobilized to provide a forum to resolve disputes between nations. The U.N. can be the place where the deadly escalation of armaments of mass destruction in the Middle East can be reversed. The U.N. should be given the opportunity to provide a framework for an Arab contribution to the resolution of the Gulf crisis.

Our nation must not submit to the inevitability of war. By acting now on a very broad scale we as people of faith will mobilize on behalf of a peaceful alternative. Citizen action and the strength of public opinion could literally make possible a solution to this crisis without war.

We call upon the churches and upon the nation to fast and pray for peace, to pursue every means available of public dialogue and popular expression to find a way out of certain catastrophe, to resist the war option and help point the way to peace with justice.

At this moment, the resolution of the Gulf crisis will take a miracle. But in this season we are reminded that the Middle East is the cradle of miracles. That miracle must be acted and prayed into being.

BAGHDAD

Rt. Rev. Edmond L. Browning, New York, NY
Presiding Bishop, The Episcopal Church

Rev. Joan Brown Campbell, New York, NY
General Secretary-elect, National Council of Churches

Rev. Dr. Milton B. Efthimiou, New York, NY
Greek Orthodox Archdiocese of North and South America

Rev. Dr. Fred Lofton, Memphis, TN
Immediate Past President, Progressive National Baptist Convention, Inc.
Representing Dr. Charles Adams, President, Progressive National Baptist Convention, Inc.

Rev. Dr. Edwin G. Mulder, New York, NY
General Secretary, Reformed Church in America

Bishop MELVIN G. TALBERT, San Francisco, CA
California-Nevada Annual Conference, United Methodist Church

JIM WALLIS, Washington, D.C.
Sojourners Magazine

Rev. Dr. DANIEL E. WEISS, Valley Forge, PA
General Secretary, American Baptist Churches in the USA

JERUSALEM

Bishop HERBERT W. CHILSTROM, Chicago, IL
Bishop, Evangelical Lutheran Church in America

Bishop VINTON ANDERSON, St. Louis, MO
Moderator, Black Church Liaison Committee of the World Council of Churches

Rev. MAC CHARLES JONES, Kansas City, MO
Representing Dr. E. E. Jones, President, National Baptist Convention of America

Rev. Dr. DONALD E. MILLER, Elgin, IL
General Secretary, Church of the Brethren

Dr. PATRICIA J. RUMER, New York, NY
General Director, Church Women United

Rev. Dr. ROBERT STEPHANOPOULOS, New York, NY
Standing Conference of Canonical Orthodox Bishops in the Americas
Dean of the Greek Orthodox Archdiocesan Cathedral of the Holy Trinity
Greek Orthodox Archdiocese of North and South America

Rev. ANGELIQUE WALKER-SMITH, Trenton, NJ
Representing Dr. Franklyn Richardson, General Secretary, National Baptist Convention, USA, Inc.

BEIRUT

Rev. Dr. JAMES E. ANDREWS, Louisville, KY
Stated Clerk, Presbyterian Church (USA)

Very Rev. LEONID KISHKOVSKY, Syosset, NY
President, National Council of Churches

Rev. Dr. PAUL SHERRY, Cleveland, OH
President, United Church of Christ

7. *Message From Thirty-two Church Leaders to President Bush*

A telegram urging a delay of military action was sent to President George Bush by thirty-two church leaders on January 15, 1991.

MR. PRESIDENT,

We stand today on the verge of a military engagement whose dimensions are ominous and unforeseeable, and whose consequences for the peoples of the Gulf, the Middle East, our own nation, and the world as a whole are unfathomable. Once begun, it is unlikely that this battle can be contained in either scope, intensity, or time. And this we know out of bitter experience: in the paths of these armies will be ground to death aggressors and victims alike; the Kuwaiti lives, national dignity, and property which you deployed troops to rescue are likely to be destroyed; and very many of our own beloved countrymen and women will die. This sacrifice is out of proportion to any conceivable gain which might be achieved through military action.

We beseech you: do not lead our nation into this abyss.

Has the United States "used all appropriate diplomatic and other means to obtain compliance by Iraq with the United Nations Security Council resolutions," as the joint resolution of Congress requires you to determine? Can the human spirit and imagination be so limited? Has the will of the nations to cause Iraq to abide by international law through strict enforcement of economic sanctions been sufficiently tested?

We beseech you: before it is too late, delay military action, give peace another chance.

The Very Rev. LEONID KISHKOVSKY, Syosset, NY
President, National Council of Churches

JAMES A. HAMILTON, New York, NY
General Secretary, National Council of Churches

The Rev. JOAN BROWN CAMPBELL, New York, NY
General Secretary Elect, National Council of Churches

Father GABRIEL H. A. ABDELSAYED, Jersey City, NJ
Coptic Orthodox Church in North America

Dr. CHARLES ADAMS, Detroit, MI
Progressive National Baptist Convention, Inc.

The Rev. Dr. JAMES E. ANDREWS, Louisville, KY
Presbyterian Church (USA)

The Rt. Rev. EDMOND L. BROWNING, New York, NY
Episcopal Church

The Rt. Rev. BISHOP CHRISTOPHER, Sewickley, PA
Serbian Orthodox Church in the U.S.A. and Canada

Elder NICHOLAS C. CHUN, Los Angeles, CA
Korean Presbyterian Church in America

Bishop HERBERT W. CHILSTROM, Chicago, IL
Evangelical Lutheran Church in America

The Rev. Dr. MILTON B. EFTHIMIOU, New York, NY
(Representative of the Most Rev. Archbishop Iakovos)
Greek Orthodox Archdiocese of North and South America

Bishop ANDREW HARSANYI, Hopatcong, NJ
Hungarian Reformed Church in America

Bishop J. CLINTON HOGGARD, Washington, DC
African Methodist Episcopal Zion Church

The Rev. Dr. JOHN O. HUMBERT, Indianapolis, IN
Christian Church (Disciples of Christ)

The Rev. Dr. THEODORE J. JEMISON, Baton Rouge, LA
National Baptist Convention U.S.A., Inc.

The Rev. Dr. E. EDWARD JONES, Shreveport, LA
National Baptist Convention of America

The Rev. Dr. DONALD E. MILLER, Elgin, IL
Church of the Brethren

The Rev. EDWIN G. MULDER, New York, NY
Reformed Church in America

Dr. PATRICIA J. RUMER, New York, NY
General Director, Church Women United

The Most Rev. Metropolitan PHILIP SALIBA, Englewood, NJ
Antiochian Orthodox Christian Church

Archbishop Mar ATHANASIUS Y. SAMUEL, Lodi, NJ
Syrian Orthodox Church of Antioch

The Rev. Dr. PAUL SHERRY, Cleveland, OH
United Church of Christ

The Rev. Dr. J. RALPH SHOTWELL, Palos Heights, IL
International Council of Community Churches

Dr. RONALD J. SIDER, Philadelphia, PA
Executive Director, Evangelicals for Social Action

The Rev. Dr. GORDON L. SOMMERS, Bethlehem, PA
Moravian Church in America

EDWIN STAUDT III, Philadelphia, PA
Philadelphia Yearly Meeting/Religious Society of Friends

The Most Rev. JOHN S. SWANTEK, Scranton, PA
Polish National Catholic Church of America

The Rev. RICHARD H. TAFEL, JR., Fort Myers Beach, FL
The Swedenborgian Church

Bishop MELVIN G. TALBERT, San Francisco, CA
The United Methodist Church

The Most Rev. METROPOLITAN THEODOSIUS, Syosset, NY
The Orthodox Church in America

Mr. JIM WALLIS, Editor, Washington, DC
Sojourners Magazine

The Rev. Dr. DANIEL E. WEISS, Valley Forge, PA
American Baptist Churches in the U.S.A.

8. Address by President Bush to National Religious Broadcasters

The President delivered this address on January 28, 1991, to the annual convention of the National Religious Broadcasters, meeting in Washington, D.C.

THIS MARKS the fifth time that I've addressed the annual convention of the National Religious Broadcasters. And once again let me say it is, for both Barbara and me, an honor to be back here.

Let me begin by congratulating you on your theme of "Declaring His Glory to All Nations." It's a theme eclipsing denominations and which reflects many of the eternal teachings in the Scripture. I speak, of course, of the teachings which uphold moral values like tolerance, compassion, faith and courage. They remind us that while God can live without man, man cannot live without God. His love and his justice inspire in us a yearning for faith and a compassion for the weak and oppressed as well as the courage and conviction to oppose tyranny and injustice.

And I'm very grateful for that resolution that has just been read prior to my speaking here.

Matthew also reminds us in these times that the meek shall inherit the earth. At home these values imbue the policies which you and I support. Like me, you endorse adoption, not abortion. And last year you helped ensure that the options of religious-based child care will not be restricted or eliminated by the federal government.

And I commend your concern, your heartfelt concern, on behalf of Americans with disabilities and your belief that students who go to school to nourish their minds should also be allowed to nourish their souls. And I have not lessened my commitment to restoring voluntary prayer in our schools.

These actions can make America a kinder and gentler place because they reaffirm the values that I spoke of earlier—values that must be central to the lives of every individual and the life of every nation. The clergyman Richard Cecil once said, "There are two classes of the wise: the men who serve God because they have found him, and the men who seek him because they have not found him yet." Abroad, as in America, our task is to serve and seek wisely through the policies we pursue.

Nowhere is this more true than in the Persian Gulf where, despite protestations of Saddam Hussein, it is not Iraq against the United States; it's the regime of Saddam Hussein against the rest of the world. Saddam tried to cast this conflict as a religious war. But it has nothing to do with religion per se. It has, on the other hand, everything to do with what religion embodies—good vs. evil, right vs. wrong, human dignity and freedom vs. tyranny and oppression.

The war in the Gulf is not a Christian war, a Jewish war or a Muslim war—it is a just war. We're told that the principles of a just war originated with classical Greek and Roman philosophers like Plato and Cicero. And later they were expounded by such Christian theologians as Ambrose, Augustine, Thomas Aquinas.

The first principle of a just war is that it support a just cause. Our cause could not be more noble. We seek Iraq's withdrawal from Kuwait—completely, immediately and without condition, the restoration of Kuwait's legitimate government and the security and stability of the Gulf. We will see that Kuwait once again is free, that the nightmare of Iraq's occupation has ended and that naked aggression will not be rewarded.

We seek nothing for ourselves. As I have said, U.S. forces will leave as soon as their mission is over, as soon as they are no longer needed or desired. And let me add, we do not seek the destruction of Iraq. We have respect for the people of Iraq, for the importance of Iraq in the region. We do not want a country so destabilized that Iraq itself could be a target for aggression.

But a just war must also be declared by legitimate authority. Operation Desert Storm is supported by unprecedented U.N. solidarity, the principle of collective self-defense, twelve Security Council resolutions and, in the Gulf, twenty-eight nations from six continents united—resolute that we will not waiver and that Saddam's aggression will not stand.

I salute the aid—economic and military—from countries who have joined in this unprecedented effort—whose courage and sacrifice have inspired the world. We're not going it alone, but believe me, we are going to see it through.

Every war—every war—is fought for a reason. But a just war is fought for the right reasons—for moral, not selfish reasons. Let me take a moment to tell you a story, a tragic story, about a family whose two sons, eighteen and nineteen, reportedly refused to lower the Kuwaiti flag in front of their home. For this crime, they were executed by the Iraqis. Then, unbelievably, their parents were asked to pay the price of the bullets used to kill them.

Some ask whether its moral to use force to stop the rape, the pillage, the plunder of Kuwait. And my answer: Extraordinary diplomatic efforts having been exhausted to resolve the matter peacefully, then the use of force is moral.

A just war must be a last resort. As I have often said, we did not want war. But you all know the verse from Ecclesiastes: there is "a time for peace, a time for war." From August 2, 1990—last summer, August 2—to January 15, 1991—166 days—we tried to resolve this conflict. Secretary of State Jim Baker made an extraordinary effort to achieve peace. More than 200 meetings with foreign dignitaries, ten diplomatic missions, six congressional appearances. Over 103,000 miles traveled to talk with, among others, members of the United Nations, the Arab League and the European Community. And sadly, Saddam Hussein rejected out of hand every overture made by the United States and by other countries as well. He made this just war an inevitable war.

We all know that war never comes easy or cheap. War is never without the loss of innocent life. And that is war's greatest tragedy. But when a war must be fought for the greater good, it is our gravest obligation to conduct a war in proportion to the threat. And that is why we must keep casualties to a minimum. And we've done so. I'm very proud of our military in achieving this end.

From the very first day of the war, the allies have waged war against Saddam's military. We are doing everything possible, believe me, to avoid hurting the innocent. Saddam's response? Wanton, barbaric bombing of civilian areas. America and her allies value life. We pray that Saddam Hussein will see reason. To date, his indiscriminate use of those Scud missiles—nothing more than weapons of terror; they have no military—they can offer no military advantage, weapons of terror—it outraged the world what he has done.

The price of war is always high. And so it must never, ever be undertaken without total commitment to a successful outcome. It is only justified when victory can be achieved. I have pledged that this will not be another Vietnam. And let me assure you here today, it won't be another Vietnam.

We are fortunate, we are very fortunate to have in this crisis the finest armed forces ever assembled. An all-volunteer force, joined by courageous allies. And we will prevail because we have the finest soldiers, sailors, airmen, Marines and Coast Guardsmen that any nation has ever had.

But above all, we will prevail because of the support of the American people, armed with a trust in God and in the principles that make men free. People like each of you in this room. I salute the Voice of Hope's live radio programming for U.S. and allied troops in the Gulf. And your Operation Desert Prayer and worship services for our troops held by, among others, the man who over a week ago led a wonderful prayer service at Fort Myer over here across the river in Virginia, the Rev. Billy Graham.

America has always been a religious nation—perhaps never more than now. Just look at the last several weeks. Churches, synagogues, mosques reporting record attendance at services. Chapels packed during working hours as Americans stop in for a moment or two. Why? To pray for peace. And I know—of course, I know—that some disagree with the course that I've taken, and I have no bitterness in my heart about that at all, no anger. I am convinced that we are doing the right thing. And tolerance is a virtue, not a vice.

But with the support and prayers of so many there can be no question in the minds of our soldiers or in the minds of our enemy about what Americans think. We know that this is a just war. And we know that, God willing, this is a war we will win. But most of all, we know that ours would not be the land of the free if it were not also the home of the brave. No one wanted war less than I did. No one is more determined to seize from battle the real peace that can offer hope, that can create a new world order.

When this war is over, the United States, its credibility restored, will have a key leadership role in helping to bring peace to the rest of the Middle East. And I have been honored to serve as president of this great nation for two years now and believe more than ever that one cannot be America's president without trust in God. I cannot imagine a world, a life, without the presence of the One through whom all things are possible.

During the darkest days of the Civil War, a man we revere not merely for what he did, but what he was, was asked whether he thought the Lord was on his side. And, said Abraham Lincoln, "My concern is not whether God is on our side, but whether we are on God's side." My fellow Americans, I firmly believe in my heart of hearts that time will soon be on the side of peace because the world is overwhelmingly on the side of God.

Thank you for this occasion. And may God bless our great country. And may we remember—and please remember all of our coalition's armed forces in your prayers. Thank you and God bless you.

9. Statement by Jim Wallis

Jim Wallis, editor of the religious monthly Sojourners *and pastor of the Sojourners community in Washington, D.C., released this statement entitled "This War Cannot Be Justified" on February 1, 1991.*

PRESIDENT Bush and his religious backers assert that the war in the Persian Gulf is a "just war." Indeed, every war in the history of this country has been called "just" by the president who waged it. It should come as no surprise that President Bush is now wrapping himself in the mantle of religion and morality as he pursues war in the Middle East.

But the war with Iraq cannot be justified on moral grounds. In resurrecting the language of moral discourse, the president and his theological advisers have failed to address the fundamental moral questions that have been at stake in this conflict since the beginning.

For more than five months before the war began, the America people wrestled with those questions in an unprecedented public debate, only to have them disappear in the illuminated skies over Baghdad. But the media's fascination with military technology, the collapse of congressional dissent, and the official pronouncement of this war's righteousness will not erase the basic moral contradictions of the Gulf crisis. The moral issues did not go away the day the fighting started. Indeed, they have become even more urgent and alarming.

To have put infinitely more energy and will into a military buildup than into political diplomacy in the Gulf crisis is a moral issue. This is not a war of "last resort," as the president has claimed. The many days and miles of shuttle diplomacy to which the president has referred were overwhelmingly directed toward building a military coalition against Saddam Hussein and authorizing its use rather than a serious attempt to deal with the underlying disputes and grievances at stake in the Gulf and, indeed, the whole region.

From the beginning, ultimatums substituted for negotiations and mutual threats pre-empted substantive dialogue. Without compromising on Iraq's withdrawal from Kuwait, there were and still are alternatives to war that address the underlying issues. The outbreak of war reveals a profound failure of political leadership on all sides. To now justify military conflict by claiming the failure of diplomacy is to compound the moral failure.

To unleash the demons of war in the Middle East is a moral issue. It risks engulfing the region in volatility, bitterness, ecological disaster, the possible use of chemical and nuclear weapons, and violence that will only multiply and reverberate around the Middle East and the world in the days ahead—and likely even for generations to come. George Bush has backed us into the corner of war with Saddam Hussein. And to back a dictator as dangerous and brutal as Saddam into such a corner, rather than to contain, undercut and defeat him in other ways, is a serious political and moral miscalculation.

In this crisis the United States is reaping what it has sown. For President Bush to justify the war as necessary to "protect our way of life"—a way of life in which six percent of the world's population consumes more than twenty-five percent of the world's oil—is a moral issue. The lack of an energy policy in the West that honors our responsibilities to both justice and the environment is a moral failure.

For the West to have so long controlled and manipulated the Arab world on the basis of an insatiable thirst for oil is a moral issue. Oil is still the real motivator in this crisis and has created a fundamental moral hypocrisy. If there were not oceans of oil beneath the Kuwaiti sands, would we be at war in the Gulf today? The United States has not acted out of President Bush's "conviction to oppose injustice" in myriad countries around the globe, from El Salvador to South Africa, from Haiti to Cambodia. In fact, in many cases, the United States has not only refused to oppose tyranny and aggression, but has been both a passive and an active supporter of repressive regimes—including Saddam Hussein's.

Should we declare war on China and begin bombing Beijing for its crushing of the democracy movement and its brutal invasion and occupation of neighboring Tibet? Should we bomb Moscow for the Soviet Union's violent repression of independence movements in the Baltics? The massive U.S. response to aggression and injustice in Kuwait, while virtually ignoring it or even supporting it in so many other cases, is a moral double standard.

In particular, to have so long accepted and supported the injustice done to Palestinians through twenty-three years of brutal occupation underlies this conflict and is a moral issue. Just because Saddam Hussein has sought to use the Palestinian question for his own self-serving purposes does not diminish its importance on its own moral grounds. To delay further the legitimate grievances of Palestinians in order not to reward Saddam Hussein's aggression is morally unacceptable.

To undertake one of the greatest aerial bombardments in history is a moral issue of yet unknown proportions. We have confirmed reports of civilian casualties from refugees who have been eyewitnesses to the bombing and from church sources in the region. Destruction of homes, schools, hospitals, and churches are an ominous harbinger of human suffering yet to come.

To send hundreds of thousands of young Americans into battle is an issue of great moral consequence. We must all continue to support the American women and men in uniform. But as many of the families of soldiers in the Gulf have pleaded, the best way to support our troops is to bring them home physically safe and psychologically whole. It is crucial to begin to separate our support for the soldiers from support for the war and return to the fundamental moral questions that underlie this conflict.

That U.S. troops are disproportionately people of color reflects the moral injustice of this nation's continued racial polarization. It is a moral contradiction that young people, whose door to a better life is closed at home, have been promised an open door to the future through military careers and education only to see that open door now become a pathway to killing or being killed.

The cost of this war at home is a moral issue. Our cities suffer the ravages of poverty and neglect while the military consumes more than a billion dollars a day in the Middle East. The bombs exploding in the Middle East also are exploding in many of our own neighborhoods, again deferring the hope of justice at home.

Bush claims that we are contributing to a new world order by intervening on Kuwait's behalf. But to turn away from the non-military instruments of sanctions, diplomacy, and multilateral political resolve in favor of the technology of war forestalls the hope of a genuinely new world order by again affirming the principles of the old world order—that "might makes right." And in Kuwait, as in Vietnam, it is possible that we may again be witnessing a U.S. campaign that destroys a country in order to save it.

Despite the claims of political leaders, our choices are not simply inaction or war, appeasement or conflagration. This war has been created by political leaders with limited vision and abundant technology. And a last-minute, just war defense is merely a cynical replacement for persistent diplomacy and moral reflection.

In his address to the National Religious Broadcasters Convention [see document 8], President Bush claimed that the forces of the world arrayed with us against Iraq are on God's side. But are we? When Gabriel Habib, general secretary of the Middle East Council of Churches, was recently asked by the BBC, "Whose side is God on in this war?" his response was, "God is on the side of the suffering."

God's blessing cannot be invoked either for George Bush's moral crusade or Saddam Hussein's holy war. The true face of God is always revealed in compassion for those who suffer in war the consequences of human failure.

10. A Call to the Churches

The following statement signed by more than 140 church leaders was released simultaneously on February 12, 1991, in New York and Washington and in Canberra, Australia, at the Seventh Assembly of the World Council of Churches. The text and list of signatories are taken from the copy sent out by the Communication Unit of the National Council of Churches.

THE CHURCHES have been at the forefront of those urging peaceful alternatives to war in the Middle East. We said, "War is not the answer" [see document 6]. We have wrestled with our varied theological traditions, returning to fundamental questions of the Christian faith. We agreed that the stakes in human lives were so high, and the potential for catastrophe in a Middle East war so great, that military confrontation had to be averted. Even in victory, there would be no winners in this war. War would bring nothing but loss to us all and unleash violence that would only multiply and reverberate around the region and the world in the days ahead—and likely even for generations to come. We have insisted that there are alternatives to war and have indicated what they could be.

But now the nation is at war—a war that should have been avoided. And a great human tragedy of yet unknown proportions has begun to unfold. When Gabriel Habib, General Secretary of the Middle East Council of Churches, was recently asked by a BBC reporter, "Whose side is God on in this war?" his response was, "God is on the side of the suffering."

Already many people are suffering: young American servicemen and women being sent into battle and their fearful families at home; people of color who are a disproportionate number of those doing the fighting, even while many of their families still fight for survival at home; Kuwaitis enduring brutal occupation; Iraqi families living under the daily rain of bombardment; Israeli parents putting gas masks on their children under the terror of missile attack; Palestinians and other Arabs who see their hopes for dignity and freedom dimmed by the clouds of war; prisoners of war paraded on our television screens; Iraqi draftees being carpet-bombed in the desert; the thousands of refugees who are already fleeing for their lives.

It is for the sake of these—and the many more who will follow—that we opposed this war on moral grounds and remain opposed to it now. On their behalf we call for a halt to the fighting—a ceasefire—and a fresh effort to find a diplomatic solution.

We call upon our churches across the country to open their doors and their hearts in a time of national trauma and to reach across international boundaries to our brothers and sisters in the Middle East who are also in great crisis.

Let our churches reach out in a spirit of dialogue and seek ways to bring Muslims, Christians, and Jews together to address our fears, concerns and hopes for peace.

Let our churches exercise their pastoral and prophetic ministry by becoming places of comfort and calm sanctuary in the midst of the "Desert Storm" of war, thus reclaiming the historic tradition of providing "safe shelter" in times of trouble.

Let our churches be havens of prayer, silence and meditation throughout the week for those who seek the peace of Christ in the midst of media bombardment and the political noise that surrounds us.

Let our churches offer prayers of intercession for wisdom

and compassion on the part of political leaders on all sides of this conflict, and for mercy and justice for war's many victims.

Let our churches provide pastoral support for military personnel, comfort and hope for their families, friends, and communities as they grapple with their fear, confusion and grief.

Let our churches stand ready to help those returning from war with physical, psychological, economic and spiritual wounds and needs.

Let our churches offer support and assistance to conscientious objectors who are refusing military service for reasons of faith and conscience, and to those who cannot obey military orders that conflict with the church's teachings on the sacredness of human life.

Let our churches become places for reasoned discussion and spiritual discernment for those wrestling with the moral issues at stake in this crisis, and for those seeking both a deeper understanding of the Middle East and a Christian response to modern warfare.

Let our churches give voice to the cries for justice of those silenced by grinding poverty and inequality in our own society, of those who will pay the price of this war not only in dreams deferred but in the denial of basic human needs.

Let our churches embrace the bereaved, maimed and homeless of the Middle East through a generous response to the ministry of compassion.

Let our churches become centers for nonviolence, preparing people to act and to respond to conflict in ways that take seriously the gospel mandate to love one another.

Let Christians help build a disciplined, morally-based nonviolent movement in response to the war in the Gulf and in response to poverty and suffering throughout the world.

The words of the gospel cannot be reconciled with what is now happening in the Gulf. It is on Jesus' call to be peacemakers that we are united and will take our stand.

We, the undersigned, make this call. We invite others to join.

LEADERS OF THE NATIONAL COUNCIL OF CHURCHES (U.S.A.)

The Very Rev. LEONID KISHKOVSKY, President, National Council of Churches

JAMES A. HAMILTON, General Secretary, National Council of Churches

The Rev. JOAN BROWN CAMPBELL, General Secretary-Elect, NCC

Fr. GABRIEL H. A. ABDELSAYED, Coptic Orthodox Church in North America

Dr. CHARLES ADAMS, Progressive National Baptist Convention, Inc.

Bishop VINTON R. ANDERSON, African Methodist Episcopal Church

The Rev. JAMES ANDREWS, Presbyterian Church (U.S.A.)

The Rt. Rev. Bishop KHAJAG BARSAMIAN, Diocese of the Armenian Church of America

Bishop RICHARD O. BASS, Christian Methodist Episcopal Church

The Most Rev. EDMOND L. BROWNING, The Episcopal Church

Bishop JOHN BRYANT, African Methodist Episcopal Church

Bishop HERBERT CHILSTROM, Evangelical Lutheran Church in America

Bishop CAESAR COLEMAN, Christian Methodist Episcopal Church

Fr. MILTON EFTHIMIOU, Greek Orthodox Archdiocese of North America

Bishop J. CLINTON HOGGARD, African Methodist Episcopal Zion Church

The Rev. JOHN HUMBERT, Christian Church (Disciples of Christ)

The Rev. Dr. E. EDWARD JONES, National Baptist Convention of America

STEPHEN MAIN, Friends United Meeting

ARCHBISHOP MAKARY, Patriarchal Parishes — Russian Orthodox Church
The Rev. DONALD E. MILLER, Church of the Brethren
The Rev. EDWIN G. MULDER, Reformed Church in America
The Most. Rev. Metropolitan PHILIP SALIBA, Antiochian Orthodox Christian Archdiocese
BISHOP SAMUEL, Syrian Orthodox Patriarchate of Antioch
The Rev. PAUL SHERRY, United Church of Christ
The Rev. J. RALPH SHOTWELL, International Council of Community Churches
The Rev. GORDON L. SOMMERS, Moravian Church in America (Northern Province)
The Most Rev. JOHN SWANTEK, Polish National Catholic Church
Bishop MELVIN G. TALBERT, United Methodist Church
Bishop FREDERICK TALBOT, African Methodist Episcopal Church
The Rev. DANIEL WEISS, American Baptist Churches

ROMAN CATHOLIC BISHOPS

Bishop CHARLES A. BUSWELL, Diocese of Pueblo, CO (retired)
Bishop NICHOLAS D'ANTONIO, Archdiocese of New Orleans
Bishop MAURICE J. DINGMAN, Diocese of Des Moines, IA (retired)
Bishop JOHN J. FITZPATRICK, Diocese of Brownsville, TX
Bishop JOSEPH A. FRANCIS, Archdiocese of Newark
Bishop THOMAS J. GUMBLETON, Archdiocese of Detroit, President, Pax Christi, USA
Archbishop RAYMOND G. HUNTHAUSEN, Archdiocese of Seattle
Bishop IBRAHIM IBRAHIM, Chaldean Catholic Bishop of the U.S.
Bishop JOSEPH L. IMESCH, Diocese of Joliet, IL
Bishop MICHAEL H. KENNY, Diocese of Juneau, AK
Bishop RAYMOND A. LUCKER, Diocese of New Ulm, MN
Bishop LEROY T. MATTHIESEN, Diocese of Amarillo, TX
Bishop WILLIAM SKYLSTAD, Diocese of Spokane, WA
Bishop JOHN J. SNYDER, Diocese of St. Augustine, FL
Bishop WALTER SULLIVAN, Diocese of Richmond, VA

OTHER RELIGIOUS LEADERS

Dr. DALE BISHOP, National Council of Churches
BONNIE BLOCK, Lutheran Peace Fellowship

The Rev. RICHARD L. DEATS, Fellowship of Reconciliation
SHELLY DOUGLASS, Ground Zero for Nonviolent Action
The Rev. ARMIN HEIDMAN, Lutheran Peace Fellowship
Dr. KATHLEEN S. HURTY, National Council of Churches
DON MOSLEY, Jubilee Partners
Dr. PATRICIA RUMER, Church Women United
The Rev. EMORY SEARCY, National Clergy and Laity Concerned
The Rev. KEN SEHESTED, Baptist Peace Fellowship of North America
Dr. RON SIDER, Evangelicals for Social Action
The Rev. DONALD WAGNER, Mercy Corps International
JIM WALLIS, *Sojourners*

AMERICANS ATTENDING THE SEVENTH ASSEMBLY OF THE WORLD COUNCIL OF CHURCHES
[Seventy names appeared here.]

OTHER ROMAN CATHOLIC LEADERS
[Fifteen names appeared here.]

Notes

Part One: James Turner Johnson

1. For a fuller discussion of the presence of the just war tradition in American culture, see James Turner Johnson, "The Just War Idea and the American Search for Peace," pp. 69–101 in George Weigel and John P. Langan, S.J., eds., *The American Search for Peace* (Washington, D.C.: Georgetown University Press, 1991).

2. *Time*, Feb. 11, 1991, p. 42; cf. the State of the Union Message, text in the *New York Times*, Jan. 30, 1991, p. A 12.

3. Archbishop Daniel Pilarczyk, "Letter to President Bush: The Persian Gulf Crisis," *Origins* 20:25 (Nov. 29, 1990), p. 399.

4. Archbishop John Roach, "Debate on the Persian Gulf: Essential Questions," *Origins* 20:28 (Dec. 20, 1990), pp. 457–60.

5. *The Christian Century*, Feb. 6–13, 1991, pp. 134–35.

6. National Conference of Catholic Bishops, *The Challenge of Peace* (Washington, D.C.: U.S. Catholic Conference, 1983), para. 80.

7. James Turner Johnson, *The Quest for Peace* (Princeton and Guildford, Surrey: Princeton University Press, 1987), pp. 3–47, 91–127, 162–70.

8. See, for example, John Howard Yoder, *What Would You Do?* (Scottdale, PA, and Kitchener, Ont.: Herald Press, 1983) and *When War Is Unjust* (Minneapolis: Augsburg Publishing House, 1984); Stanley Hauerwas, "A Pacifist Response to the Bishops," pp. 149–82 in Paul Ramsey, *Speak Up for Just War or Pacifism* (University Park and London: Pennsylvania State University Press).

9. Paul Ramsey, *The Just War* (New York: Charles Scribner's, 1968), p. 5.

10. Paul Ramsey, "A Political Ethics Context for Strategic Thinking," in Morton A. Kaplan, *Strategic Thinking and Its Moral Implications* (Chicago: University of Chicago Center for Policy Study, 1973), pp. 124–25.

11. See James Turner Johnson, *Ideology, Reason, and the Limitation of War* (Princeton and London: Princeton University Press, 1975) and *Just War Tradition and the Restraint of War* (Princeton and Guildford, Surrey: Princeton University Press, 1981), parts two and three.

12. James F. Childress, "Just War Theories: The Bases, Interrelations, Priorities, and Functions of Their Criteria," *Theological Studies* 39 (Sept. 1978), pp. 427–45.

13. Paul Ramsey, *War and the Christian Conscience* (Durham, NC: Duke University Press, 1961).

14. Ramsey, *The Just War*, see especially chaps. 7, 11, and 17.

15. *Ibid.*, chap. 5, pp. 131ff.; chap. 10, pp. 189–92.

16. See James Turner Johnson, "Just War in the Thought of Paul Ramsey," *The Journal of Religious Ethics* 19:2 (Fall 1991), pp. 183–207.

17. Walter Stein, *Nuclear Weapons and Christian Conscience* (London: Merlin Press, 1965) and John Finnis, Joseph Boyle, and Germain Grisez, *Nuclear Deterrence, Morality and Realism* (Oxford: Clarendon Press, 1987).

18. See, for example, Ronald H. Stone and Dana Wilbanks, eds., *The Peacemaking Struggle: Militarism and Resistance* (Lanham, MD: University Press of America, 1985).

19. J. Bryan Hehir, "The New Nuclear Debate: Political and Ethical Considerations," pp. 35–95 in Robert A. Gessert and J. Bryan Hehir, *The New Nuclear Debate* (New York: Council on Religion and International Affairs, 1976), p. 47.

20. See Jeffrey Stout, "Ramsey and Others on Nuclear Ethics," *The Journal of Religious Ethics* 19:2 (Fall 1991), pp. 209–37.

21. National Conference of Catholic Bishops, *The Challenge of Peace*, paras. 85–110.

22. The historical sources define seven *ius ad bellum* criteria (just cause, right authority, right intention, overall proportionality of good to evil, reasonable hope of success, last resort, and the goal of peace) and two criteria for the *ius in bello* (discrimination or noncombatant immunity and proportionality of means). Different thinkers develop these concepts in different ways, sometimes clearly subordinating some criteria to others. For my own reconstruction of the criteria and their meanings see below and the discussion in Johnson, *Just War Tradition*, pp. xxi–xxiv; compare William V. O'Brien, *The Conduct of Just and Limited War* (New York: Praeger, 1981), chaps. 1 and 2.

23. See note 6 above.

24. On this development see James Brown Scott, *The Spanish Origin of International Law* (Oxford: Clarendon Press; London: Humphrey Milford, 1934); Johnson, *Just War Tradition*, pp. 75–103.

25. Tom J. Farer, "The Laws of War 25 Years after Nuremberg," *International Conciliation*, no. 583 (May 1971), pp. 14–17.

26. Cf. John Locke, *An Essay Concerning the True Original, Extent and End of Civil Government*, sections 197–93, and my discussion of this passage in Johnson, *Ideology, Reason, and the Limitation of War*, pp. 235–40.

27. Cf. Grotius, *De Jure Belli ac Pacis* (*Of the Law of War and Peace*), books I and II, chaps. I and XXII–XXVI.

28. See Johnson, *Just War Tradition*, chap. VII; cf. O'Brien, *The Conduct of Just and Limited War*, chaps. 9, 13, and 14.

29. U.S. Air Force, *International Law: The Conduct of Armed Conflict and Air Operations, 19 November 1976*, Air Force Pamphlet AFP 110–31 (Washington, D.C.: Headquarters of the Air Force, 1976), chaps. 1, 5–6.

30. Paul Fussell, *The Great War and Modern Memory* (New York and London: Oxford University Press, 1975); Michael Herr, *Dispatches* (New York: Avon Books, 1978).

31. Augustine, *Quaestiones in Heptateuchum* 6.10.

32. Thomas Aquinas, *Summa Theologiae* II/II, question 40, article 1.

33. Augustine, *Contra Faustum* XXII.74.

34. Prominent examples, all from the field of religion, include Archbishop Roach's testimony on behalf of the Catholic bishops and Dale Bishop's testimony on behalf of the National Council of Churches before the Senate Foreign Relations Committee on December 6, the November 15 "Message and Resolution on the Gulf and Middle East Crisis" of the National Council of Churches, and the October 5 statement of the presiding bishop of the Episcopal Church on the Gulf crisis. For a fuller discussion of the reaction of American religious bodies see George Weigel's chapter in this volume. See also the documents in Part Three.

35. For a postwar judgment on the destruction wrought by the air war against Iraq see "Effects of War Begin to Fade in Iraq," *New York Times*, Sunday, May 12, 1991, sect. 4, p. 2.

36. O'Brien, *The Conduct of Just and Limited War*, chap. 1.

37. For discussion of this tradition see Johnson, *The Quest for Peace*, chap. IV.

38. "Newly Confident Hussein Takes Show on the Road," *New York Times*, May 7, 1991, pp. A1, A17.

PART TWO: GEORGE WEIGEL

1. On the demographic decline of liberal Protestantism, cf. Wade Clark Roof and William McKinney, *American Mainline Religion: Its Changing Shape and Future* (New Brunswick: Rutgers University Press, 1987). On the radicalization of these churches in their interface with the public policy arena, cf. K.L. Billingsley, *From Mainline to Sideline: The Social Witness of the National Council of Churches* (Washington: Ethics and Public Policy Center, 1990).

2. In the light of these phenomena, Richard John Neuhaus has suggested that this is the "Catholic moment" in America, which for our purposes here means the "moment in which the Roman Catholic Church in the United States assumes its rightful role in the culture-forming task of constructing a religiously informed public philosophy for the American experiment in ordered liberty" [Richard John Neuhaus, *The Catholic Moment: The Paradox of the Church in the Postmodern World* (San Francisco: Harper and Row, 1987, p. 283)]. How far American Catholicism's formal

religious leadership is from seizing this opportunity will become clearer as this essay unfolds.

3. For a pathbreaking analysis of the Religious New Right, cf. Richard John Neuhaus, *The Naked Public Square: Religion and Democracy in America* (Grand Rapids: Wm. B. Eerdmans, 1984).

4. Cf. Richard Land, "The Crisis in the Persian Gulf and 'Just Wars,'" *Commentary* #079, Christian Life Commission of the Southern Baptist Convention, Dec. 21, 1990. Land's column was reprinted in Baptist state newspapers across the country.

5. Cf., for example, "On Just Wars: An Interview with Michael Walzer," *Tikkun* 6:1, pp. 40–42.

6. Cf. "A Message to the Member Communions of the National Council of Churches of Christ in the U.S.A. Regarding the Crisis in the Gulf," in *Pressing for Peace: The Churches Act in the Gulf Crisis* (New York: NCC-USA, 1991), pp. 2–5. The text of this message is reprinted in full in Part Three of this volume (document 1).

7. Cf. "A Message and Resolution on the Gulf and Middle East Crisis," in *Pressing for Peace*, pp. 7–11. The text of this message is reprinted in Part Three of this volume (document 3).

8. Bishop Talbert was quoted in a Religious News Service wire story dated Dec. 7, 1990.

9. Cf. "War Is Not the Answer: A Message to the American People," in *Pressing for Peace*, pp. 14–17. The text of this message is reprinted in Part Three of this volume (document 6).

10. Cf. "Delay Military Action, Give Peace a Chance: A Message to President Bush from American Church Leaders," in *Pressing for Peace*, pp. 20–22. The text of this message is reprinted in Part Three of this volume (document 7).

11. This point was not lost on Abdul Amir Al-Anbari, the Iraqi ambassador to the U.N., who said in a Nov. 29 Security Council debate:

> I wish to give you one picture of the support for our viewpoint which we have received. This is reflected in the statement by the National Council of Churches in the United States. They represent 42 million American citizens. In the middle of November, they . . . stressed the need to hold an international conference to deal with the Palestinian/Israeli conflict. They have accused the American administration of duplicity and hypocrisy because they are calling for the withdrawal of Iraqi forces according to Security Council resolutions in total disregard for the need for requesting the withdrawal of Israeli forces in the occupied territories in the West Bank, Jerusalem, Sinai, Jordan, and South Lebanon. The Council of Churches have reaffirmed in their statement, and I quote, "the region cries out for a U.S. policy that seeks to address all the causes of injustice including those of Israel, Palestine, Lebanon, and Cyprus." The question that must be raised now is the following: Will the Security Council rise to the level of responsibility for imposing a just and lasting peace through an integrated approach dealing with all the problems in that region? Your response to this question constitutes your historic mission.

12. The Czechoslovakian statement, dated Dec. 17, 1990, was translated and circulated by RCDA-Research Center for Religion and Human Rights in Closed Societies, and reprinted in the Feb. 11, 1991, issue of *National Review*, p. 15.

13. The Mahony letter may be found in *Origins* 20:24 (Nov. 22, 1990), pp. 384–86. The Pilarczyk letter may be found in *Origins* 20:25 (Nov. 29, 1990), pp. 397, 399–400. The Roach testimony may be found in *Origins* 20:28 (Dec. 20, 1990), pp. 457–60. All three documents are also reprinted in Part Three of this volume (documents 2, 4, and 5).

14. The Pax Christi statement was signed by Archbishop Hunthausen of Seattle; by Bishops Buswell (emeritus of Puebla), D'Antonio (auxiliary of New Orleans), Dingman (emeritus of Des Moines), Gumbleton (auxiliary of Detroit), Kenny (Juneau), Murphy (auxiliary of Baltimore), Untener (Saginaw), Schoenherr (auxiliary of Detroit), and Sullivan (Richmond); and by Abbot Edward McCorkell of the Trappists in Virginia.

15. Bishop Curlin's homily was quoted in *The Catholic Standard* (Washington, D.C.), 41:3 (Jan. 17, 1991), pp. 1, 5.

16. Bishop Sullivan was quoted in Thomas Mullen, "Catholics in Military Told to Be Conscientious," *Richmond News-Leader*, Jan. 7, 1991, pp. 9, 15.

17. The *Civiltà Cattolica* editorial was reported in the Jan. 6, 1991, issue of the *National Catholic Register*. The original may be found in *La Civiltà Cattolica*, Nov. 17, 1991.

18. *Theological Studies* 5 (1944), 261–309.

19. "Another Failure in a Bankrupt Foreign Policy," *The Christian Century*, April 17, 1991, p. 419.

20. Cf. Richard D. Parry, "The Gulf War and the Just War Doctrine," *America*, April 20, 1991, pp. 442–45.

21. Bernard Lewis, "At Stake in the Gulf," *New York Review of Books*, Nov. 21, 1990, p. 46.

22. *Ibid.*

23. NCC news release, Feb. 28, 1991.

24. Cf. S. Robert Lichter, Daniel Amundson, and Linda S. Lichter, *Media Coverage of the Catholic Church* (Washington: Center for Media and Public Affairs, 1991).

25. Thomas Michel, S.J., "Why the War Bodes Ill for Christian-Muslim Relations," *Origins* 20:39 (March 7, 1991), p. 636.

26. *Ibid.*, p. 637.

27. *Ibid.*, p. 635.

28. *Ibid.*

29. *Ibid.*, p. 636.

30. *Ibid.*, p. 638.

31. *Ibid.*, pp. 637–38.

32. *Nostra Aetate*, 3.

33. Cf. the measured comments of Cardinal Francis Arinze, president of the Pontifical Council for Inter-Religious Dialogue, in an interview in *30*

Days, March 1989, pp. 14–15. A far more stringent appraisal of the prospects for Christian-Islamic dialogue may be found in the same issue of the same journal, in an essay by Bishop Adolphe-Marie Hardy of Beauvais, France (p. 16).

The Holy See made clear, throughout the Gulf War, its concern that the war not be construed as one between Christianity and Islam. It should also be noted that, during the war, Pope John Paul II issued a new encyclical on Christian mission, *Redemptoris Missio*, which challenged Islamic countries on issues of religious liberty.

34. On a related front, far more critical attention should also have been paid by the relevant authorities to the comments during the war of Patriarch Raphael I Bidawid, the Chaldean-rite patriarch of Baghdad. While in Rome, shortly after the beginning of the air war, Patriarch Bidawid told the *National Catholic Register*, "We are all Iraqi citizens. . . . We have to support our president because he is our president and the country is our country" (*National Catholic Register*, Feb. 3, 1991). Such a position, of course, has no foundation whatsoever in Catholic ethics. But the patriarch's support for Saddam Hussein was of a piece with his defense of Scud attacks on civilian population centers in Israel, and his claim that "this entire war has been planned" by the Israelis.

35. *Apostolicam Actuositatem* (Decree on the Apostolate of the Laity), 14 (emphasis added).

36. Albert Camus, *Neither Victims Nor Executioners* (New York: Continuum, 1980).

Index of Names

Abraham, 82
Air Force, U.S., AFP 11–31 manual, 17–18
Ambrose, 142
America, 65
American Society of Christian Ethics, 4
Amnesty International, 56
Anabaptist tradition, 86
Aquinas, Saint Thomas, 21, 71, 142
Arab League, 144
Arabs, 38, 56, 67, 69, 72–76, 78–83, 94, 109, 123, 127–28, 132, 134, 148, 154
Arafat, Yasir, 69, 77
Aspin, Les, 59
Augustine, Saint, 21, 24, 142
Augustinian realism, 71, 86
Aziz, Tariq, 60

Baghdad, 33, 64, 147
Baker, James, 58, 60, 99, 111, 113, 119–20, 122, 143–44
Baltic states, 149
BBC, 151, 153
Beijing, 149
Bentham, Jeremy, 37
Browning, Edmond Lee, 45
Brussels Declaration of 1874, 13
Brzezinski, Zbigniew, 59
Bush administration, 48, 52, 61, 100, 121
Bush, Barbara, 141
Bush, George, 4, 38, 54–55, 59–61, 95, 106, 111, 113–14, 119, 137, 141, 147–51

Cambodia, 149
Camus, Albert, 90
Catholic bishops, 11–12, 46, 58, 89, 99, 114, 117, 120; *see also* National Conference of Catholic Bishops
Catholic Church, 46–51, 58–59, 62–68, 72, 80, 84–86, 99–100, 113–14, 117–18, 120, 122
Cecil, Richard, 142
Central America, 76
Central Europe, 69, 83, 88
Challenge of Peace, The, 11–12, 114
Chesterton, G. K., 45
Childress, James, 8
China, 149
Christian Century, The, 4, 65
Christian Realism, 50, 85
Church Leaders' Peace Pilgrimage to the Middle East, 52, 54–55, 58, 131

Church World Service and Witness, 93
Cicero, 142
Civiltà Cattolica, La, 63–64, 79
Civil War, 145
Clausewitz, Karl von, 28
Coast Guard, 144
Cold War, vii, 36, 41, 49–50, 63, 67–68, 77, 79, 86, 127
Congregational churches, 45
Congress, 5, 23, 49, 61, 67, 101, 110–11, 125
Constantine, 65
Constitution, 23
Crowe, William, 59
Crucé, 37
Curlin, William, 62
Cyprus, 107–8, 110, 133

Declaration on . . . Non-Christian Religions (Vatican II), 82
Desert Shield, Desert Storm, *see* Operation Desert . . .
Dugan, Michael, 33

Eastern Europe, 69, 83, 88
Egypt, 56, 67, 72, 108
El Salvador, 76, 149
Episcopal Church, 45
European Community, 144

Fahd, King, 80
Falwell, Jerry, 47
Farer, Tom J., 13
Finnis, John, 11
First Amendment, 46
Ford, John, 64
France, 60
French Revolution, 15
Fussell, Paul, 19

Gadhafi, Moammar, 80
Gaza Strip, 56, 133
Geneva Conventions, 13
Geneva talks, 30, 60
Germany, 34
Graham, Billy, 145
Grand Mufti of Jerusalem, 77
Grotius, Hugo, 14
Gumbleton, Thomas, 59

Habib, Gabriel, 151, 153
Hague Conferences, 13
Haifa, 76
Haiti, 149
Haram al-Sharif/Temple Mount, 108
Havel, Václav, 83
Hehir, J. Bryan, 11
Henry, Carl F. H., 47
Herr, Michael, 19
Hitler, Adolf, 77
Hobbes, Thomas, 63
House Armed Services Committee, 59

International Organization for Migration, 96, 98
Iran, 32, 38, 133
Islam, 78–80, 82–85
Israel, 34, 38–39, 53, 69, 72, 74, 76–78, 97, 108, 110, 127, 132–33, 154

Jama'at-i-Islami movement, 80
Japan, 34, 40
Jerusalem, 132
Jesuits, 63, 65, 79
Jews, American, 46, 48, 71
Jordan, 38–39, 54, 74, 93, 96, 108, 133

Jordan Valley Development Authority, 74
Judaism, 79
Just War, The (Ramsey), 9
"Just War Tradition and the War in the Gulf" (*Christian Century*), 4

Kant, Immanuel, 36
Khomeini, Ayatollah, 80
Korea, 54
Kurds, 39, 66, 78

Land, Richard, 47
Latin America, 79
League of Nations, 15, 36
Lebanon, 74, 108, 110, 133
Levant, 71
Lewis, Bernard, 69
Libya, 56
Lincoln, Abraham, 146
Luther, Martin, 83

Mahony, Roger, 58, 59–61, 99, 113–14, 117, 120
Marines, 144
Marxism, 57
Methodist churches, 45
Michel, Thomas, 79–84
Middle Ages, 16, 21, 24
Middle East Council of Churches, 93, 96, 110–11, 151
Mohammed, 82
Moscow, 149
Murray, John Courtney, 50, 85
Muslim Brotherhood, 80
Muslims, 71, 76, 82, 132, 142, 154

Napoleonic Wars, 15
Nasser, Gamal Abdel, 81
National Catholic Reporter, 61
National Conference of Catholic Bishops, 4, 47–48, 59, 61–62, 89, 111, 113; *see also* Catholic bishops
National Council of Churches, viii, 47–48, 50–58, 61, 64–67, 76–77, 88–89, 93–94, 97, 107, 109–11, 131; Communication Unit, 153; Executive Coordinating Committee, 52, 93, 97, 106; General Board, 105, 110
National Religious Broadcasters, 4, 141, 150–51
National Shrine of the Immaculate Conception, 62
Network, 51
New Testament, 46
New York Times, 5
Nicaragua, 51, 71, 76
Niebuhr, Reinhold, 9, 50, 85
Nostra Aetate, 82
Nuremberg trials, 13, 15

O'Brien, William V., 36, 49
Old Testament, 46
"On the Morality of Obliteration Bombing" (Ford), 64
OPEC, 73
Operation Desert Prayer, 145
Operation Desert Shield, 45, 132, 143, 154
Operation Desert Storm, 31, 45, 48, 55
Origins, 79
Orthodox churches, 54

Pact of Paris, 15
Palestine, 38, 53, 72, 97, 108, 110
Palestine Liberation Organization, 39, 56, 69, 77

Palestinians, 67, 74, 76–77, 79, 132, 149, 154
Pan-Arabism, 80
Parry, Richard D., 65
Pax Christi, 59, 61–62
Penn, William, 37
Perez de Cuellar, Javier, 57, 60
Pilarczyk, Daniel, 4, 59–61, 113, 119
Plato, 142
Presbyterian churches, 45
Protestants, conservative/evangelical, 46–47, 111; liberal, 50, 65, 86; mainline/oldline, 45–46, 48–49, 54–55, 66–67, 72, 74–77, 84–85

Qur'an, 83

Rainbow Coalition, 51
Ramsey, Paul, 6, 8–11, 13, 21, 34, 41, 48, 50, 85
Reformation, 6
Republican Party, 45
Revolution of 1989, vii, 51, 88
Roach, John, 4, 59–61, 89, 117

Saint-Pierre, Jacques, 37
Sandinistas, 51, 76
Saudi Arabia, 34, 38–39, 56, 67, 80, 94, 106, 108, 123, 129
Scud missiles, 34, 76, 144
Second Vatican Council, 82, 88, 102
Senate Foreign Relations Committee, 4, 59, 89, 117
Shi'ites, 39, 66, 78
Small Catechism (Luther), 83
Sojourners, 50, 58, 147
South Africa, 149
Southern Baptist Convention, 47
Soviet Union, 34, 67, 77, 102, 149
Stein, Walter, 10–11
Sullivan, Walter, 62
Sully, Maximilien, 37
Sylvester, Nancy, 51
Syria, 39, 133

Tabligh movement, 80
Talbert, Melvin, 53–54
Tel Aviv, 76
Temple Mount, 108
Tercermundismo, 50, 79
Texaco, 69
Third World, 69, 80
Thomistic tradition, 86
Tibet, 149
Tokyo trials, 15
Tomahawk cruise missile, 64
Turkey, 107

United Nations, 15–16, 22–23, 27, 36, 40–41, 52, 55–57, 60, 67, 95, 98, 100–102, 106–7, 109–11, 114, 125–26, 128, 132–33, 143; Security Council, 5, 16, 22–23, 36, 41, 56–57, 61, 67, 93–98, 107, 110–11, 137, 143
United Nations Charter, 16, 22–23, 111
United States Catholic Conference, viii, 47, 61, 79, 89, 99, 117, 119–20
Universal Declaration on Human Rights, 84

Vatican, 63, 79, 82
Vietnam War, 8, 11, 19–20, 32–35, 52, 54, 66, 68, 70, 95, 106, 144, 150
Voice of Hope, 145

Wallis, Jim, 48, 58, 78, 147
War and the Christian Conscience (Ramsey), 8–9, 34
"War Is Not the Answer," 131
War Powers Act, 23
Wesleyan tradition, 86
West Bank, 56, 133
West Germany, 40
Wilsonian moralism, 71, 78, 87
World Council of Churches, 111, 153
World War I, 15, 36
World War II, 13, 15, 19–20, 32–36, 63, 69, 77, 81, 90

Yemen, 56

Zionism, 39

This index was compiled by intern Lawrence Florio.